A Memoir of
Jane Austen

‿

Illustrated & Annotated
A 200th Anniversary Edition

J.E. AUSTEN LEIGH

Solis Press

'He knew of no one but himself who was inclined to the work. This is no uncommon motive. A man sees something to be done, knows of no one who will do it but himself, and so is driven to the enterprise.'
Helps' *Life of Columbus*, ch. i.

Publisher's note: Annotations by George Cavendish are indicated by the use of square brackets.

Photo credit:
p. 141, Rudi Riet, http://creativecommons.org/licenses/ by-sa/2.0/ (cropped and converted to monochrome)

The second edition of *A Memoir of Jane Austen* was originally published in 1871 by Richard Bentley & Son. This edition completely reset with minor changes, annotations and illustrations is published in 2017 by Solis Press

ISBN: 978-1-910146-68-2

Published by Solis Press, PO Box 482,
Tunbridge Wells TN2 9QT, Kent, England

Web: www.solispress.com | *Twitter*: @SolisPress

Contents

List of illustrations

---

1 [There is some dispute as to whether this painting is of the famous novelist or of one of her nieces. It is also uncertain as to whether it was painted by J. Zoffany.]

Preface

THE MEMOIR OF MY[2] Aunt, Jane Austen, has been received with more favour than I had ventured to expect. The notices taken of it in the periodical press, as well as letters addressed to me by many with whom I am not personally acquainted, show that an unabated interest is still taken in every particular that can be told about her. I am thus encouraged not only to offer a Second Edition of the *Memoir*, but also to enlarge it with some additional matter which I might have scrupled to intrude on the public if they had not thus seemed to call for it. In the present Edition, the narrative is somewhat enlarged, and a few more letters are added; with a short specimen of her childish stories. The cancelled chapter of *Persuasion* is given, in compliance with wishes both publicly and privately expressed. Extracts are given from a novel which she had begun a few months before her death. I regret that the little which I have been able to add could not appear in my First Edition; as much of it was either unknown to me, or not at my command, when I first published; and I hope that I may claim some indulgent allowance for the difficulty of recovering little facts and feelings which had been merged half a century deep in oblivion.

November 17, 1870.

---

2 [James Edward Leigh Austen, 1798–1874, was son of James Austen, 1765–1819, eldest brother of Jane.]

JANE AUSTEN (painted by J. Zoffany)

Chapter I

Introductory Remarks—Birth of Jane Austen—Her Family
Connections—Their Influence on her Writings.

MORE THAN HALF A century has passed away since I, the youngest of the mourners,[3] attended the funeral of my dear aunt Jane
in Winchester Cathedral; and now, in my old age, I am asked whether
my memory will serve to rescue from oblivion any events of her life
or any traits of her character to satisfy the enquiries of a generation of
readers who have been born since she died. Of events her life was sin-
gularly barren: few changes and no great crisis ever broke the smooth
current of its course. Even her fame may be said to have been posthumous: it did not attain to any vigorous life till she had ceased to
exist. Her talents did not introduce her to the notice of other writers,
or connect her with the literary world, or in any degree pierce through
the obscurity of her domestic retirement. I have therefore scarcely any
materials for a detailed life of my aunt; but I have a distinct recollection
of her person and character; and perhaps many may take an interest in
a delineation, if any such can be drawn, of that prolific mind whence
sprung the Dashwoods and Bennets, the Bertrams and Woodhouses,
the Thorpes and Musgroves, who have been admitted as familiar guests
to the firesides of so many families, and are known there as individu-
ally and intimately as if they were living neighbours. Many may care
to know whether the moral rectitude, the correct taste, and the warm
affections with which she invested her ideal characters, were really
existing in the native source whence those ideas flowed, and were actually exhibited by her in the various relations of life. I can indeed bear
witness that there was scarcely a charm in her most delightful characters that was not a true reflection of her own sweet temper and loving
heart. I was young when we lost her; but the impressions made on the
young are deep, and though in the course of fifty years I have forgotten
much, I have not forgotten that 'Aunt Jane' was the delight of all her
nephews and nieces. We did not think of her as being clever, still less as

---

3 I went to represent my father, who was too unwell to attend himself, and thus I was
the only one of my generation present. [James Austen died 13 December 1819.]

being famous; but we valued her as one always kind, sympathising, and amusing. To all this I am a living witness, but whether I can sketch out such a faint outline of this excellence as shall be perceptible to others may be reasonably doubted. Aided, however, by a few survivors[4] who knew her, I will not refuse to make the attempt. I am the more inclined to undertake the task from a conviction that, however little I may have to tell, no one else is left who could tell so much of her.

Jane Austen was born on December 16, 1775, at the Parsonage House of Steventon in Hampshire. Her father, the Rev. George Austen, was of a family long established in the neighbourhood of Tenterden and Sevenoaks in Kent. I believe that early in the seventeenth century they were clothiers. Hasted, in his history of Kent, says: 'The clothing business was exercised by persons who possessed most of the landed property in the Weald, insomuch that almost all the ancient families of these parts, now of large estates and genteel rank in life, and some of them ennobled by titles, are sprung from ancestors who have used this great staple manufacture, now almost unknown here.' In his list of these families Hasted places the Austens, and he adds that these clothiers 'were usually called the Gray Coats of Kent; and were a body so numerous and united that at county elections whoever had their vote and interest was almost certain of being elected.' The family still retains a badge of this origin; for their livery is of that peculiar mixture of light blue and white called Kentish gray, which forms the facings of the Kentish militia.

Mr. George Austen had lost both his parents before he was nine years old. He inherited no property from them; but was happy in having a kind uncle, Mr. Francis Austen, a successful lawyer at Tunbridge,[5] the ancestor of the Austens of Kippington, who, though he had children of his own, yet made liberal provision for his orphan nephew. The boy received a good education at Tunbridge School, whence he obtained a

---

4 My chief assistants have been my sisters, Mrs. B. Lefroy and Miss Austen, whose recollections of our aunt are, on some points, more vivid than my own. I have not only been indebted to their memory for facts, but have sometimes used their words. Indeed some passages towards the end of the work were entirely written by the latter.

I have also to thank some of my cousins, and especially the daughters of Admiral Charles Austen, for the use of letters and papers which had passed into their hands, without which this memoir, scanty as it is, could not have been written.

5 [Nowadays spelled Tonbridge. Not to be confused with nearby Tunbridge Wells.]

scholarship, and subsequently a fellowship, at St. John's College, Oxford. In 1764 he came into possession of the two adjoining Rectories of Deane and Steventon in Hampshire; the former purchased for him by his generous uncle Francis, the latter given by his cousin Mr. Knight. This was no very gross case of plurality, according to the ideas of that time, for the two villages were little more than a mile apart, and their united populations scarcely amounted to three hundred. In the same year he married Cassandra, youngest daughter of the Rev. Thomas Leigh, of the family of Leighs of Warwickshire, who, having been a fellow of All Souls, held the College living of Harpsden, near Henley-upon-Thames. Mr. Thomas Leigh was a younger brother of Dr. Theophilus Leigh, a personage well known at Oxford in his day, and his day was not a short one, for he lived to be ninety, and held the Mastership of Balliol College for above half a century. He was a man more famous for his sayings than his doings, overflowing with puns and witticisms and sharp retorts; but his most serious joke was his practical one of living much longer than had been expected or intended. He was a fellow of Corpus, and the story is that the Balliol men, unable to agree in electing one of their own number to the Mastership, chose him, partly under the idea that he was in weak health and likely soon to cause another vacancy. It was afterwards said that his long incumbency had been a judgment on the Society for having elected an *Out-College Man*.[6] I imagine that the front of Balliol towards Broad Street which has recently been pulled down must have been built, or at least restored, while he was Master, for the Leigh arms were placed under the cornice at the corner nearest to Trinity gates. The beautiful building lately erected has destroyed this record, and thus 'monuments themselves memorials need.'

His fame for witty and agreeable conversation extended beyond the bounds of the University. Mrs. Thrale, in a letter to Dr. Johnson, writes thus: 'Are you acquainted with Dr. Leigh,[7] the Master of Balliol College, and are you not delighted with his gaiety of manners and youthful vivacity, now that he is eighty-six years of age? I never heard a more perfect or excellent pun than his, when some one told him how, in a late dispute among the Privy Councillors, the Lord Chancellor struck the

6 There seems to have been some doubt as to the validity of this election; for Hearne says that it was referred to the Visitor, who confirmed it. (Hearne's *Diaries*, vol. 2.)
7 Mrs. Thrale writes Dr. *Lee*, but there can be no doubt of the identity of person.

table with such violence that he split it. "No, no, no," replied the Master; "I can hardly persuade myself that he *split* the *table*, though I believe he *divided* the *Board*."'

Some of his sayings of course survive in family tradition. He was once calling on a gentleman notorious for never opening a book, who took him into a room overlooking the Bath Road, which was then a great thoroughfare for travellers of every class, saying rather pompously, 'This, Doctor, I call my study.' The Doctor, glancing his eye round the room, in which no books were to be seen, replied, 'And very well named too, sir, for you know Pope[8] tells us, "The proper *study* of mankind is *Man*." ' When my father went to Oxford he was honoured with an invitation to dine with this dignified cousin. Being a raw undergraduate, unaccustomed to the habits of the University, he was about to take off his gown, as if it were a great coat, when the old man, then considerably turned eighty, said, with a grim smile, 'Young man, you need not strip: we are not going to fight.' This humour remained in him so strongly to the last that he might almost have supplied Pope with another instance of 'the ruling passion strong in death,' for only three days before he expired, being told that an old acquaintance was lately married, having recovered from a long illness by eating eggs, and that the wits said that he had been egged on to matrimony, he immediately trumped the joke, saying, 'Then may the yoke sit easy on him.' I do not know from what common ancestor the Master of Balliol and his greatniece Jane Austen, with some others of the family, may have derived the keen sense of humour which they certainly possessed.

Mr. and Mrs. George Austen resided first at Deane, but removed in 1771 to Steventon, which was their residence for about thirty years. They commenced their married life with the charge of a little child, a son of the celebrated Warren Hastings, who had been committed to the care of Mr. Austen before his marriage, probably through the influence of his sister, Mrs. Hancock, whose husband at that time held some office under Hastings in India. Mr. Gleig, in his *Life of Hastings*, says that his son George, the offspring of his first marriage, was sent to England in 1761 for his education, but that he had never been able to ascertain to whom this precious charge was entrusted, nor what became of him. I

---

8 [Alexander Pope, 1688–1744, an English poet. The quotation that follows in the text is from 'An Essay on Man', 1733–4.]

am able to state, from family tradition, that he died young, of what was then called putrid sore throat; and that Mrs. Austen had become so much attached to him that she always declared that his death had been as great a grief to her as if he had been a child of her own.

About this time, the grandfather of Mary Russell Mitford, Dr. Russell, was Rector of the adjoining parish of Ashe; so that the parents of two popular female writers must have been intimately acquainted with each other.

As my subject carries me back about a hundred years, it will afford occasions for observing many changes gradually effected in the manners and habits of society, which I may think it worth while to mention. They may be little things, but time gives a certain importance even to trifles, as it imparts a peculiar flavour to wine. The most ordinary articles of domestic life are looked on with some interest, if they are brought to light after being long buried; and we feel a natural curiosity to know what was done and said by our forefathers, even though it may be nothing wiser or better than what we are daily doing or saying ourselves. Some of this generation may be little aware how many conveniences, now considered to be necessaries and matters of course, were unknown to their grandfathers and grandmothers. The lane between Deane and Steventon has long been as smooth as the best turnpike road; but when the family removed from the one residence to the other in 1771, it was a mere cart track, so cut up by deep ruts as to be impassable for a light carriage. Mrs. Austen, who was not then in strong health, performed the short journey on a feather-bed, placed upon some soft articles of furniture in the waggon which held their household goods. In those days it was not unusual to set men to work with shovel and pickaxe to fill up ruts and holes in roads seldom used by carriages, on such special occasions as a funeral or a wedding. Ignorance and coarseness of language also were still lingering even upon higher levels of society than might have been expected to retain such mists. About this time, a neighbouring squire, a man of many acres, referred the following difficulty to Mr. Austen's decision: 'You know all about these sort of things. Do tell us. Is Paris in France, or France in Paris? for my wife has been disputing with me about it.' The same gentleman, narrating some conversation which he had heard between the rector and his wife, represented the latter as beginning her reply to her husband with a round oath; and when his daughter called him to task, reminding him that

Mrs. Austen never swore, he replied, 'Now, Betty, why do you pull me up for nothing? that's neither here nor there; you know very well that's only *my way of telling the story*.' Attention has lately been called by a celebrated writer to the inferiority of the clergy to the laity of England two centuries ago. The charge no doubt is true, if the rural clergy are to be compared with that higher section of country gentlemen who went into parliament, and mixed in London society, and took the lead in their several counties; but it might be found less true if they were to be compared, as in all fairness they ought to be, with that lower section with whom they usually associated. The smaller landed proprietors, who seldom went farther from home than their county town, from the squire with his thousand acres to the yeoman who cultivated his hereditary property of one or two hundred, then formed a numerous class—each the aristocrat of his own parish; and there was probably a greater difference in manners and refinement between this class and that immediately above them than could now be found between any two persons who rank as gentlemen. For in the progress of civilisation, though all orders may make some progress, yet it is most perceptible in the lower. It is a process of 'levelling up;' the rear rank 'dressing up,' as it were, close to the front rank. When Hamlet mentions, as something which he had 'for *three years taken* note of,' that 'the toe of the peasant comes so near the heel of the courtier,' it was probably intended by Shakespeare as a satire on his own times; but it expressed a principle which is working at all times in which society makes any progress. I believe that a century ago the improvement in most country parishes began with the clergy; and that in those days a rector who chanced to be a gentleman and a scholar found himself superior to his chief parishioners in information and manners, and became a sort of centre of refinement and politeness.

Mr. Austen was a remarkably good-looking man, both in his youth and his old age. During his year of office at Oxford he had been called the 'handsome Proctor;' and at Bath, when more than seventy years old, he attracted observation by his fine features and abundance of snow-white hair. Being a good scholar he was able to prepare two of his sons for the University, and to direct the studies of his other children, whether sons or daughters, as well as to increase his income by taking pupils.

In Mrs. Austen also was to be found the germ of much of the ability which was concentrated in Jane, but of which others of her children had a share. She united strong common sense with a lively imagination, and often expressed herself, both in writing and in conversation, with epigrammatic force and point. She lived, like many of her family, to an advanced age. During the last years of her life she endured continual pain, not only patiently but with characteristic cheerfulness. She once said to me, 'Ah, my dear, you find me just where you left me—on the sofa. I sometimes think that God Almighty must have forgotten me; but I dare say He will come for me in His own good time.' She died and was buried at Chawton, January 1827, aged eighty-eight.

💚

Her own family were so much, and the rest of the world so little, to Jane Austen, that some brief mention of her brothers and sister is necessary in order to give any idea of the objects which principally occupied her thoughts and filled her heart, especially as some of them, from their characters or professions in life, may be supposed to have had more or less influence on her writings: though I feel some reluctance in bringing before public notice persons and circumstances essentially private.

Her eldest brother James, my own father, had, when a very young man, at St. John's College, Oxford, been the originator and chief supporter of a periodical paper called *The Loiterer*, written somewhat on the plan of the *Spectator* and its successors, but nearly confined to subjects connected with the University. In after life he used to speak very slightingly of this early work, which he had the better right to do, as, whatever may have been the degree of their merits, the best papers had certainly been written by himself. He was well read in English literature, had a correct taste, and wrote readily and happily, both in prose and verse. He was more than ten years older than Jane, and had, I believe, a large share in directing her reading and forming her taste.

Her second brother, Edward, had been a good deal separated from the rest of the family, as he was early adopted by his cousin, Mr. Knight, of Godmersham Park in Kent and Chawton House in Hampshire; and finally came into possession both of the property and the name. But though a good deal separated in childhood, they were much together in after life, and Jane gave a large share of her affections to him and his children. Mr. Knight was not only a very amiable man, kind and indulgent to all connected with him, but possessed also a spirit of fun and liveliness, which made him especially delightful to all young people.

Her third brother, Henry, had great conversational powers, and inherited from his father an eager and sanguine disposition. He was a very entertaining companion, but had perhaps less steadiness of purpose, certainly less success in life, than his brothers. He became a clergyman when middle-aged; and an allusion to his sermons will be found in one of Jane's letters. At one time he resided in London, and was useful in transacting his sister's business with her publishers.

Her two youngest brothers, Francis and Charles, were sailors during that glorious period of the British navy which comprises the close of the last and the beginning of the present century, when it was impossible for an officer to be almost always afloat, as these brothers were, without seeing service which, in these days, would be considered distinguished. Accordingly, they were continually engaged in actions of more or less importance, and sometimes gained promotion by their success. Both rose to the rank of Admiral, and carried out their flags to distant stations.

Francis lived to attain the very summit of his profession, having died, in his ninety-third year, GCB.[9] and Senior Admiral of the Fleet, in 1865. He possessed great firmness of character, with a strong sense of duty, whether due from himself to others, or from others to himself. He was consequently a strict disciplinarian; but, as he was a very religious man, it was remarked of him (for in those days, at least, it was remarkable) that he maintained this discipline without ever uttering an oath or permitting one in his presence. On one occasion, when ashore in a seaside town, he was spoken of as '*the* officer who kneeled at church;' a custom which now happily would not be thought peculiar.

Charles was generally serving in frigates or sloops; blockading harbours, driving the ships of the enemy ashore, boarding gun-boats, and frequently making small prizes. At one time he was absent from England on such services for seven years together. In later life he commanded the *Bellerophon*,[10] at the bombardment of St. Jean d'Acre[11] in 1840. In 1850 he went out in the *Hastings*, in command of the East India and China station, but on the breaking out of the Burmese war he

---

9 [Knight Grand Cross of the Order of the Bath.]
10 [HMS *Bellerophon* was a 74-gun Royal Navy ship of the line. It was on this ship that Napoleon surrendered in 1815.]
11 [Nowadays called Acre, a city in northern Israel.]

transferred his flag to a steam sloop, for the purpose of getting up the shallow waters of the Irrawaddy, on board of which he died of cholera in 1852, in the seventy-fourth year of his age. His sweet temper and affectionate disposition, in which he resembled his sister Jane, had secured to him an unusual portion of attachment, not only from his own family, but from all the officers and common sailors who served under him. One who was with him at his death has left this record of him: 'Our good Admiral won the hearts of all by his gentleness and kindness while he was struggling with disease, and endeavouring to do his duty as Commander-in-chief of the British naval forces in these waters. His death was a great grief to the whole fleet. I know that I cried bitterly when I found he was dead.' The Order in Council of the Governor-General of India, Lord Dalhousie, expresses 'admiration of the staunch high spirit which, notwithstanding his age and previous sufferings, had led the Admiral to take his part in the trying service which has closed his career.'

These two brothers have been dwelt on longer than the others because their honourable career accounts for Jane Austen's partiality for the Navy, as well as for the readiness and accuracy with which she wrote about it. She was always very careful not to meddle with matters which she did not thoroughly understand. She never touched upon politics, law, or medicine, subjects which some novel writers have ventured on rather too boldly, and have treated, perhaps, with more brilliancy than accuracy. But with ships and sailors she felt herself at home, or at least could always trust to a brotherly critic to keep her right. I believe that no flaw has ever been found in her seamanship either in *Mansfield Park* or in *Persuasion*.

But dearest of all to the heart of Jane was her sister Cassandra, about three years her senior. Their sisterly affection for each other could scarcely be exceeded. Perhaps it began on Jane's side with the feeling of deference natural to a loving child towards a kind elder sister. Something of this feeling always remained; and even in the maturity of her powers, and in the enjoyment of increasing success, she would still speak of Cassandra as of one wiser and better than herself. In childhood, when the elder was sent to the school of a Mrs. Latournelle, in the Forbury at Reading, the younger went with her, not because she was thought old enough to profit much by the instruction there imparted, but because she would have been miserable without her sister; her mother observing that 'if Cassandra were going to have her head cut off, Jane would insist on sharing her fate.' This attachment was never interrupted or weakened. They lived in the same home, and shared the same bed-room, till separated by death. They were not exactly alike. Cassandra's was the colder and calmer disposition; she was always prudent and well judging, but with less outward demonstration of feeling and less sunniness of temper than Jane possessed. It was remarked in her family that 'Cassandra had the *merit* of having her temper always under command, but that Jane had the *happiness* of a temper that never required to be commanded.' When *Sense and Sensibility* came out, some persons, who knew the family slightly, surmised that the two elder Miss Dashwoods were intended by the author for her sister and herself; but this could not be the case. Cassandra's character might indeed represent the '*sense*' of Elinor, but Jane's had little in common with the '*sensibility*' of Marianne. The young woman who, before the age of twenty, could so clearly discern the failings of Marianne Dashwood, could hardly have been subject to them herself.

This was the small circle, continually enlarged, however, by the increasing families of four of her brothers, within which Jane Austen found her wholesome pleasures, duties, and interests, and beyond which she went very little into society during the last ten years of her life. There was so much that was agreeable and attractive in this family party that its members may be excused if they were inclined to live somewhat too exclusively within it. They might see in each other much to love and esteem, and something to admire. The family talk had abundance of spirit and vivacity, and was never troubled by disagreements even in little matters, for it was not their habit to dispute or argue with each other: above all, there was strong family affection and firm union, never to be broken but by death. It cannot be doubted that all this had its influence on the author in the construction of her stories, in which a family party usually supplies the narrow stage, while the interest is made to revolve round a few actors.

It will be seen also that though her circle of society was small, yet she found in her neighbourhood persons of good taste and cultivated minds. Her acquaintance, in fact, constituted the very class from which she took her imaginary characters, ranging from the member of parliament, or large landed proprietor, to the young curate or younger midshipman of equally good family; and I think that the influence of these early associations may be traced in her writings, especially in two particulars. First, that she is entirely free from the vulgarity, which is so offensive in some novels, of dwelling on the outward appendages of wealth or rank, as if they were things to which the writer was unaccustomed; and, secondly, that she deals as little with very low as with very high stations in life. She does not go lower than the Miss Steeles, Mrs. Elton, and John Thorpe, people of bad taste and underbred manners, such as are actually found sometimes mingling with better society. She has nothing resembling the Brangtons, or Mr. Dubster and his friend Tom Hicks, with whom Madame D'Arblay[12] loved to season her stories, and to produce striking contrasts to her well-bred characters.

---

12 [The marriage name of Frances ('Fanny') Burney, 1752–1840, an English novelist.]

Chapter II

Description of Steventon—Life at Steventon—Changes of
Habits and Customs in the last Century.

As the first twenty-five years, more than half of the brief life of Jane Austen, were spent in the parsonage of Steventon, some description of that place ought to be given. Steventon is a small rural village upon the chalk hills of north Hants, situated in a winding valley about seven miles from Basingstoke. The South-Western railway crosses it by a short embankment, and, as it curves round, presents a good view of it on the left hand to those who are travelling down the line, about three miles before entering the tunnel under Popham Beacon. It may be known to some sportsmen, as lying in one of the best portions of the Vine Hunt. It is certainly not a picturesque country; it presents no grand or extensive views; but the features are small rather than plain. The surface continually swells and sinks, but the hills are not bold, nor the valleys deep; and though it is sufficiently well clothed with woods and hedgerows, yet the poverty of the soil in most places prevents the timber from attaining a large size. Still it has its beauties. The lanes wind along in a natural curve, continually fringed with irregular borders of native turf, and lead to pleasant nooks and corners. One who knew and loved it well very happily expressed its quiet charms, when he wrote

> True taste is not fastidious, nor rejects,
> Because they may not come within the rule
> Of composition pure and picturesque,
> Unnumbered simple scenes which fill the leaves
> Of Nature's sketch book.

Of this somewhat tame country, Steventon, from the fall of the ground, and the abundance of its timber, is certainly one of the prettiest spots; yet one cannot be surprised that, when Jane's mother, a little before her marriage, was shown the scenery of her future home, she should have thought it unattractive, compared with the broad river, the rich valley, and the noble hills which she had been accustomed to behold at her native home near Henley-upon-Thames.

The house itself stood in a shallow valley, surrounded by sloping meadows, well sprinkled with elm trees, at the end of a small village of cottages, each well provided with a garden, scattered about prettily on either side of the road. It was sufficiently commodious to hold pupils in addition to a growing family, and was in those times considered to be above the average of parsonages; but the rooms were finished with less elegance than would now be found in the most ordinary dwellings. No cornice marked the junction of wall and ceiling; while the beams which supported the upper floors projected into the rooms below in all their naked simplicity, covered only by a coat of paint or whitewash: accordingly it has since been considered unworthy of being the Rectory house of a family living, and about forty-five years ago it was pulled down for the purpose of erecting a new house in a far better situation on the opposite side of the valley.

North of the house, the road from Deane to Popham Lane ran at a sufficient distance from the front to allow a carriage drive, through turf and trees. On the south side the ground rose gently, and was occupied by one of those old-fashioned gardens in which vegetables and flowers are combined, flanked and protected on the east by one of the thatched mud walls common in that country, and overshadowed by fine elms. Along the upper or southern side of this garden, ran a terrace of the finest turf, which must have been in the writer's thoughts when she described Catharine Morland's childish delight in 'rolling down the green slope at the back of the house.'

But the chief beauty of Steventon consisted in its hedgerows. A hedgerow, in that country, does not mean a thin formal line of quickset, but an irregular border of copse-wood and timber, often wide enough to contain within it a winding footpath, or a rough cart track. Under its shelter the earliest primroses, anemones, and wild hyacinths were to be found; sometimes, the first bird's-nest; and, now and then, the unwelcome adder. Two such hedgerows radiated, as it were, from the parsonage garden. One, a continuation of the turf terrace, proceeded westward, forming the southern boundary of the home meadows; and was formed into a rustic shrubbery, with occasional seats, entitled 'The Wood Walk.' The other ran straight up the hill, under the name of 'The Church Walk,' because it led to the parish church, as well as to a fine old manor-house, of Henry VIII's time, occupied by a family named Digweed, who have for more than a century rented it, together with the chief farm in the parish. The church itself—I speak of it as it then was, before the improvements made by the present rector—

> A little spireless fane,
> Just seen above the woody lane,

might have appeared mean and uninteresting to an ordinary observer; but the adept in church architecture would have known that it must have stood there some seven centuries, and would have found beauty in the very narrow early English windows, as well as in the general proportions of its little chancel; while its solitary position, far from the hum of the village, and within sight of no habitation, except a glimpse of the gray manor-house through its circling screen of sycamores, has in it something solemn and appropriate to the last resting-place of the silent dead. Sweet violets, both purple and white, grow in abundance beneath its south wall. One may imagine for how many centuries the ancestors of those little flowers have occupied that undisturbed, sunny nook, and may think how few living families can boast of as ancient a tenure of their land. Large elms protrude their rough branches; old hawthorns shed their annual blossoms over the graves; and the hollow yew-tree must be at least coeval with the church.

But whatever may be the beauties or defects of the surrounding scenery, this was the residence of Jane Austen for twenty-five years. This was the cradle of her genius. These were the first objects which inspired her young heart with a sense of the beauties of nature. In strolls along those wood-walks, thick-coming fancies rose in her mind, and gradually assumed the forms in which they came forth to the world. In that simple church she brought them all into subjection to the piety which ruled her in life, and supported her in death.

The home at Steventon must have been, for many years, a pleasant and prosperous one. The family was unbroken by death, and seldom visited by sorrow. Their situation had some peculiar advantages beyond those of ordinary rectories. Steventon was a family living. Mr. Knight, the patron, was also proprietor of nearly the whole parish. He never resided there, and consequently the rector and his children came to be regarded in the neighbourhood as a kind of representatives of the family. They shared with the principal tenant the command of an excellent manor, and enjoyed, in this reflected way, some of the consideration usually awarded to landed proprietors. They were not rich, but, aided by Mr. Austen's powers of teaching, they had enough to afford a good education to their sons and daughters, to mix in the best society of the neighbourhood, and to exercise a liberal hospitality to their own

relations and friends. A carriage and a pair of horses were kept. This
might imply a higher style of living in our days than it did in theirs.
There were then no assessed taxes. The carriage, once bought, entailed
little further expense; and the horses probably, like Mr. Bennet's, were
often employed on farm work. Moreover, it should be remembered that
a pair of horses in those days were almost necessary, if ladies were to
move about at all; for neither the condition of the roads nor the style
of carriage-building admitted of any comfortable vehicle being drawn
by a single horse. When one looks at the few specimens still remaining
of coach-building in the last century, it strikes one that the chief object
of the builders must have been to combine the greatest possible weight
with the least possible amount of accommodation.

The family lived in close intimacy with two cousins, Edward and
Jane Cooper, the children of Mrs. Austen's eldest sister, and Dr. Cooper,
the vicar of Sonning, near Reading. The Coopers lived for some years
at Bath, which seems to have been much frequented in those days
by clergymen retiring from work. I believe that Cassandra and Jane
sometimes visited them there, and that Jane thus acquired the intimate
knowledge of the topography and customs of Bath, which enabled her
to write *Northanger Abbey* long before she resided there herself. After
the death of their own parents, the two young Coopers paid long visits
at Steventon. Edward Cooper did not live undistinguished. When an
undergraduate at Oxford, he gained the prize for Latin hexameters on
'Hortus Anglicus' [13] in 1791; and in later life he was known by a work on
prophecy, called *The Crisis*, and other religious publications, especially
for several volumes of Sermons, much preached in many pulpits in my
youth. Jane Cooper was married from her uncle's house at Steventon, to
Captain, afterwards Sir Thomas Williams, under whom Charles Austen
served in several ships. She was a dear friend of her namesake, but was
fated to become a cause of great sorrow to her, for a few years after the
marriage she was suddenly killed by an accident to her carriage.

There was another cousin closely associated with them at Steventon,
who must have introduced greater variety into the family circle. This
was the daughter of Mr. Austen's only sister, Mrs. Hancock. This cousin
had been educated in Paris, and married to a Count de Feuillade, of

---

13 [Latin for 'English Garden'.]

STEVENTON RECTORY (FRONT)

Back front of Steventon Rectory. 1814

STEVENTON RECTORY (REAR)

whom I know little more than that he perished by the guillotine during the French Revolution. Perhaps his chief offence was his rank; but it was said that the charge of 'incivism,' under which he suffered, rested on the fact of his having laid down some arable land into pasture—a sure sign of his intention to embarrass the Republican Government by producing a famine! His wife escaped through dangers and difficulties to England, was received for some time into her uncle's family, and finally married her cousin Henry Austen. During the short peace of Amiens, she and her second husband went to France, in the hope of recovering some of the Count's property, and there narrowly escaped being included amongst the *détenus*.[14] Orders had been given by Buonaparte's government to detain all English travellers, but at the post-houses Mrs. Henry Austen gave the necessary orders herself, and her French was so perfect that she passed everywhere for a native, and her husband escaped under this protection.

She was a clever woman, and highly accomplished, after the French rather than the English mode; and in those days, when intercourse with the Continent was long interrupted by war, such an element in the society of a country parsonage must have been a rare acquisition. The sisters may have been more indebted to this cousin than to Mrs. La Tournelle's teaching for the considerable knowledge of French which they possessed. She also took the principal parts in the private theatricals in which the family several times indulged, having their summer theatre in the barn, and their winter one within the narrow limits of the dining-room, where the number of the audience must have been very limited. On these occasions, the prologues and epilogues were written by Jane's eldest brother, and some of them are very vigorous and amusing. Jane was only twelve years old at the time of the earliest of these representations, and not more than fifteen when the last took place. She was, however, an early observer, and it may be reasonably supposed that some of the incidents and feelings which are so vividly painted in the *Mansfield Park* theatricals are due to her recollections of these entertainments.

Some time before they left Steventon, one great affliction came upon the family. Cassandra was engaged to be married to a young clergyman.

---

14 [Inmates or those being detained.]

He had not sufficient private fortune to permit an immediate union; but the engagement was not likely to be a hopeless or a protracted one, for he had a prospect of early preferment from a nobleman with whom he was connected both by birth and by personal friendship. He accompanied this friend to the West Indies, as chaplain to his regiment, and there died of yellow fever, to the great concern of his friend and patron, who afterwards declared that, if he had known of the engagement, he would not have permitted him to go out to such a climate. This little domestic tragedy caused great and lasting grief to the principal sufferer, and could not but cast a gloom over the whole party. The sympathy of Jane was probably, from her age, and her peculiar attachment to her sister, the deepest of all.

Of Jane herself I know of no such definite tale of love to relate. Her reviewer in the *Quarterly* of January 1821 observes, concerning the attachment of Fanny Price to Edmund Bertram: 'The silence in which this passion is cherished, the slender hopes and enjoyments by which it is fed, the restlessness and jealousy with which it fills a mind naturally active, contented, and unsuspicious, the manner in which it tinges every event, and every reflection, are painted with a vividness and a detail of which we can scarcely conceive any one but a female, and we should almost add, a female writing from recollection, capable.' This conjecture, however probable, was wide of the mark. The picture was drawn from the intuitive perceptions of genius, not from personal experience. In no circumstance of her life was there any similarity between herself and her heroine in *Mansfield Park*. She did not indeed pass through life without being the object of warm affection. In her youth she had declined the addresses of a gentleman who had the recommendations of good character, and connections, and position in life, of everything, in fact, except the subtle power of touching her heart. There is, however, one passage of romance in her history with which I am imperfectly acquainted, and to which I am unable to assign name, or date, or place, though I have it on sufficient authority. Many years after her death, some circumstances induced her sister Cassandra to break through her habitual reticence, and to speak of it. She said that, while staying at some seaside place, they became acquainted with a gentleman, whose charm of person, mind, and manners was such that Cassandra thought him worthy to possess and likely to win her sister's love. When they parted, he expressed his intention of soon seeing them again; and

Cassandra felt no doubt as to his motives. But they never again met. Within a short time they heard of his sudden death. I believe that, if Jane ever loved, it was this unnamed gentleman; but the acquaintance had been short, and I am unable to say whether her feelings were of such a nature as to affect her happiness.

Any description that I might attempt of the family life at Steventon, which closed soon after I was born, could be little better than a fancy-piece. There is no doubt that if we could look into the households of the clergy and the small gentry of that period, we should see some things which would seem strange to us, and should miss many more to which we are accustomed. Every hundred years, and especially a century like the last, marked by an extraordinary advance in wealth, luxury, and refinement of taste, as well as in the mechanical arts which embellish our houses, must produce a great change in their aspect. These changes are always at work; they are going on now, but so silently that we take no note of them. Men soon forget the small objects which they leave behind them as they drift down the stream of life. As Pope[15] says—

> Nor does life's stream for observation stay;
> It hurries all too fast to mark their way.

Important inventions, such as the applications of steam, gas, and electricity, may find their places in history; but not so the alterations, great as they may be, which have taken place in the appearance of our dining and drawing-rooms. Who can now record the degrees by which the custom prevalent in my youth of asking each other to take wine together at dinner became obsolete? Who will be able to fix, twenty years hence, the date when our dinners began to be carved and handed round by servants, instead of smoking before our eyes and noses on the table? To record such little matters would indeed be 'to chronicle small beer.' But, in a slight memoir like this, I may be allowed to note some of those changes in social habits which give a colour to history, but which the historian has the greatest difficulty in recovering.

At that time the dinner-table presented a far less splendid appearance than it does now. It was appropriated to solid food, rather than to flow-

---

15 [Alexander Pope's 'Of the knowledge and characters of men: An epistle to the Right Honourable Richard Lord Viscount Cobham'. The quotation should read: 'Life's Stream for Observation will not stay, / It hurries all too fast to mark their way.']

ers, fruits, and decorations. Nor was there much glitter of plate upon it; for the early dinner hour rendered candlesticks unnecessary, and silver forks had not come into general use: while the broad rounded end of the knives indicated the substitute generally used instead of them.[16]

The dinners too were more homely, though not less plentiful and savoury; and the bill of fare in one house would not be so like that in another as it is now, for family receipts were held in high estimation. A grandmother of culinary talent could bequeath to her descendant fame for some particular dish, and might influence the family dinner for many generations.

> *Dos est magna parentium*
> *Virtus.*[17]

One house would pride itself on its ham, another on its game-pie, and a third on its superior furmity, or tansey-pudding. Beer and home-made wines, especially mead, were more largely consumed. Vegetables were less plentiful and less various. Potatoes were used, but not so abundantly as now; and there was an idea that they were to be eaten only with roast meat. They were novelties to a tenant's wife who was entertained at Steventon Parsonage, certainly less than a hundred years ago; and when Mrs. Austen advised her to plant them in her own garden, she replied, 'No, no; they are very well for you gentry, but they must be terribly *costly to rear.*'

But a still greater difference would be found in the furniture of the rooms, which would appear to us lamentably scanty. There was a gener-

---

16 The celebrated Beau Brummel, who was so intimate with George IV as to be able to quarrel with him, was born in 1771. It is reported that when he was questioned about his parents, he replied that it was long since he had heard of them, but that he imagined the worthy couple must have cut their own throats by that time, because when he last saw them they were eating peas with their knives. Yet Brummel's father had probably lived in good society; and was certainly able to put his son into a fashionable regiment, and to leave him £30,000.* Raikes believes that he had been Secretary to Lord North. Thackeray's idea that he had been a footman cannot stand against the authority of Raikes, who was intimate with the son. (*Raikes's *Memoirs*, vol. ii, p. 207.) [George Bryan Brummell, 1778–1840, was the original 'Dandy' or what would be called a 'trend-setter' nowadays. He eventually fell out with 'Prinny' by asking a mutual acquaintance 'Who's your fat friend?' when referring to the Prince Regent.]

17 ['… the virtue of the parents is a large dowry', a quotation from the Roman poet Horace.]

al deficiency of carpeting in sitting-rooms, bed-rooms, and passages. A pianoforte, or rather a spinnet or harpsichord, was by no means a necessary appendage. It was to be found only where there was a decided taste for music, not so common then as now, or in such great houses as would probably contain a billiard-table. There would often be but one sofa in the house, and that a stiff, angular, uncomfortable article. There were no deep easy-chairs, nor other appliances for lounging; for to lie down, or even to lean back, was a luxury permitted only to old persons or invalids. It was said of a nobleman, a personal friend of George III and a model gentleman of his day, that he would have made the tour of Europe without ever touching the back of his travelling carriage. But perhaps we should be most struck with the total absence of those elegant little articles which now embellish and encumber our drawing-room tables. We should miss the sliding bookcases and picture-stands, the letter-weighing machines and envelope cases, the periodicals and illustrated newspapers—above all, the countless swarm of photograph books which now threaten to swallow up all space. A small writing-desk, with a smaller work-box, or netting-case, was all that each young lady contributed to occupy the table; for the large family work-basket, though often produced in the parlour, lived in the closet.

There must have been more dancing throughout the country in those days than there is now: and it seems to have sprung up more spontaneously, as if it were a natural production, with less fastidiousness as to the quality of music, lights, and floor. Many country towns had a monthly ball throughout the winter, in some of which the same apartment served for dancing and tea-room. Dinner parties more frequently ended with an extempore dance on the carpet, to the music of a harpsichord in the house, or a fiddle from the village. This was always supposed to be for the entertainment of the young people, but many, who had little pretension to youth, were very ready to join in it. There can be no doubt that Jane herself enjoyed dancing, for she attributes this taste to her favourite heroines; in most of her works, a ball or a private dance is mentioned, and made of importance.

Many things connected with the ball-rooms of those days have now passed into oblivion. The barbarous law which confined the lady to one partner throughout the evening must indeed have been abolished before Jane went to balls. It must be observed, however, that this custom was in one respect advantageous to the gentleman, inasmuch as it rendered his duties more practicable. He was bound to call upon his partner the next morning, and it must have been convenient to have only one lady for whom he was obliged

> To gallop all the country over,
> The last night's partner to behold,
> And humbly hope she caught no cold.

But the stately minuet still reigned supreme; and every regular ball commenced with it. It was a slow and solemn movement, expressive of grace and dignity, rather than of merriment. It abounded in formal bows and courtesies, with measured paces, forwards, backwards and sideways, and many complicated gyrations. It was executed by one lady and gentleman, amidst the admiration, or the criticism, of surrounding spectators. In its earlier and most palmy days, as when Sir Charles and Lady Grandison delighted the company by dancing it at their own wedding, the gentleman wore a dress sword, and the lady was armed with a fan of nearly equal dimensions. Addison observes that 'women are armed with fans, as men with swords, and sometimes do more execution with them.' The graceful carriage of each weapon was considered a test of high breeding. The clownish man was in danger of being tripped up by his sword getting between his legs: the fan held clumsily looked more of a burden than an ornament; while in the hands of an adept it could be made to speak a language of its own.[18] It was not everyone who felt qualified to make this public exhibition, and I have been told that those ladies who intended to dance minuets, used to distinguish themselves from others by wearing a particular kind of lappet on their head-dress. I have heard also of another curious proof of the respect in which this dance was held. Gloves immaculately clean were considered requisite for its due performance, while gloves a little soiled were thought good enough for a country dance; and accordingly some prudent ladies provided themselves with two pairs for their several purposes. The minuet expired with the last century: but long after

---

18 See *Spectator*, No. 102, on the Fan Exercise. Old gentlemen who had survived the fashion of wearing swords were known to regret the disuse of that custom, because it put an end to one way of distinguishing those who had, from those who had not, been used to good society. To wear the sword easily was an art which, like swimming and skating, required to be learned in youth. Children could practise it early with their toy swords adapted to their size.

it had ceased to be danced publicly it was taught to boys and girls, in order to give them a graceful carriage.

Hornpipes, cotillons, and reels, were occasionally danced; but the chief occupation of the evening was the interminable country dance, in which all could join. This dance presented a great show of enjoyment, but it was not without its peculiar troubles. The ladies and gentlemen were ranged apart from each other in opposite rows, so that the facilities for flirtation, or interesting intercourse, were not so great as might have been desired by both parties. Much heart-burning and discontent sometimes arose as to *who* should stand above *whom*, and especially as to who was entitled to the high privilege of calling and leading off the first dance: and no little indignation was felt at the lower end of the room when any of the leading couples retired prematurely from their duties, and did not condescend to dance up and down the whole set. We may rejoice that these causes of irritation no longer exist; and that if such feelings as jealousy, rivalry, and discontent ever touch celestial bosoms in the modern ball-room they must arise from different and more recondite sources.

I am tempted to add a little about the difference of personal habits. It may be asserted as a general truth, that less was left to the charge and discretion of servants, and more was done, or superintended, by the masters and mistresses. With regard to the mistresses, it is, I believe, generally understood, that at the time to which I refer, a hundred years ago, they took a personal part in the higher branches of cookery, as well as in the concoction of home-made wines, and distilling of herbs for domestic medicines, which are nearly allied to the same art. Ladies did not disdain to spin the thread of which the household linen was woven. Some ladies liked to wash with their own hands their choice china after breakfast or tea. In one of my earliest child's books, a little girl, the daughter of a gentleman, is taught by her mother to make her own bed before leaving her chamber. It was not so much that they had not servants to do all these things for them, as that they took an interest in such occupations. And it must be borne in mind how many sources of interest enjoyed by this generation were then closed, or very scantily opened to ladies. A very small minority of them cared much for literature or science. Music was not a very common, and drawing was a still rarer, accomplishment; needlework, in some form or other, was their chief sedentary employment.

But I doubt whether the rising generation are equally aware how much gentlemen also did for themselves in those times, and whether some things that I can mention will not be a surprise to them. Two homely proverbs were held in higher estimation in my early days than they are now—'The master's eye makes the horse fat;' and, 'If you would be well served, serve yourself.' Some gentlemen took pleasure in being their own gardeners, performing all the scientific, and some of the manual, work themselves. Well-dressed young men of my acquaintance, who had their coat from a London tailor, would always brush their evening suit themselves, rather than entrust it to the carelessness of a rough servant, and to the risks of dirt and grease in the kitchen; for in those days servants' halls were not common in the houses of the clergy and the smaller country gentry. It was quite natural that Catherine Morland should have contrasted the magnificence of the offices at Northanger Abbey with the few shapeless pantries in her father's parsonage. A young man who expected to have his things packed or unpacked for him by a servant, when he travelled, would have been thought exceptionally fine, or exceptionally lazy. When my uncle undertook to teach me to shoot, his first lesson was how to clean my own gun. It was thought meritorious on the evening of a hunting day, to turn out after dinner, lanthorn in hand, and visit the stable, to ascertain that the horse had been well cared for. This was of the more importance, because, previous to the introduction of clipping, about the year 1820, it was a difficult and tedious work to make a long-coated hunter dry and comfortable, and was often very imperfectly done. Of course, such things were not practised by those who had gamekeepers, and stud-grooms, and plenty of well-trained servants; but they were practised by many who were unequivocally gentlemen, and whose grandsons, occupying the same position in life, may perhaps be astonished at being told that '*such things were.*'

I have drawn pictures for which my own experience, or what I heard from others in my youth, have supplied the materials. Of course, they cannot be universally applicable. Such details varied in various circles, and were changed very gradually; nor can I pretend to tell how much of what I have said is descriptive of the family life at Steventon in Jane Austen's youth. I am sure that the ladies there had nothing to do with the mysteries of the stew-pot or the preserving-pan; but it is probable that their way of life differed a little from ours, and would have appeared to us more homely. It may be that useful articles, which would not now be produced in drawing-rooms, were hemmed, and marked, and darned in the old-fashioned parlour. But all this concerned only the outer life; there was as much cultivation and refinement of mind as now, with probably more studied courtesy and ceremony of manner to visitors; whilst certainly in that family literary pursuits were not neglected.

I remember to have heard of only two little things different from modern customs. One was, that on hunting mornings the young men usually took their hasty breakfast in the kitchen. The early hour at which hounds then met may account for this; and probably the custom began, if it did not end, when they were boys; for they hunted at an early age, in a scrambling sort of way, upon any pony or donkey that they could procure, or, in default of such luxuries, on foot. I have been told that Sir Francis Austen, when seven years old, bought on his own account, it must be supposed with his father's permission, a pony for a guinea and a half; and after riding him with great success for two seasons, sold him for a guinea more. One may wonder how the child could have so much money, and how the animal could have been obtained for so little. The same authority informs me that his first cloth suit was made from a scarlet habit, which, according to the fashion of the times, had been his mother's usual morning dress. If all this is true, the future admiral of the British Fleet must have cut a conspicuous figure in the hunting-field. The other peculiarity was that, when the roads were dirty, the sisters took long walks in pattens. This defence against wet and dirt is now seldom seen. The few that remain are banished from good society, and employed only in menial work; but a hundred and fifty years ago they were celebrated in poetry, and considered so clever a contrivance that Gay,[19] in his *Trivia*, ascribes the invention to a god stimulated by his passion for a mortal damsel, and derives the name 'Patten' from 'Patty.'

> The patten now supports each frugal dame,
> Which from the blue-eyed Patty takes the name.

But mortal damsels have long ago discarded the clumsy implement. First it dropped its iron ring and became a clog; afterwards it was fined

---

19 [John Gay, 1685–1732, English poet. The full title of the poem is *Trivia, or The Art of Walking the Streets of London*.]

down into the pliant galoshe—lighter to wear and more effectual to protect—a no less manifest instance of gradual improvement than Cowper indicates when he traces through eighty lines of poetry his 'accomplished sofa' back to the original three-legged stool.

As an illustration of the purposes which a patten was intended to serve, I add the following epigram, written by Jane Austen's uncle, Mr. Leigh Perrot, on reading in a newspaper the marriage of Captain Foote to Miss Patten:—

> Through the rough paths of life, with a patten your guard,
>   May you safely and pleasantly jog;
> May the knot never slip, nor the ring press too hard,
>   Nor the *Foot* find the *Patten* a clog.

At the time when Jane Austen lived at Steventon, a work was carried on in the neighbouring cottages which ought to be recorded, because it has long ceased to exist.

Up to the beginning of the present century, poor women found profitable employment in spinning flax or wool. This was a better occupation for them than straw plaiting, inasmuch as it was carried on at the family hearth, and did not admit of gadding and gossiping about the village. The implement used was a long narrow machine of wood, raised on legs, furnished at one end with a large wheel, and at the other with a spindle on which the flax or wool was loosely wrapped, connected together by a loop of string. One hand turned the wheel, while the other formed the thread. The outstretched arms, the advanced foot, the sway of the whole figure backwards and forwards, produced picturesque attitudes, and displayed whatever of grace or beauty the work-woman might possess.[20] Some ladies were fond of spinning, but they worked in a quieter manner, sitting at a neat little machine of varnished wood, like Tunbridge ware, generally turned by the foot, with a basin of water at hand to supply the moisture required for forming the thread, which the cottager took by a more direct and natural process from her own mouth. I remember two such elegant little wheels in our own family.

---

20 Mrs. Gaskell, in her tale of *Sylvia's Lovers*, [a novel published in 1863] declares that this hand-spinning rivalled harp-playing in its gracefulness.

It may be observed that this hand-spinning is the most primitive of female accomplishments, and can be traced back to the earliest times. Ballad poetry and fairy tales are full of allusions to it. The term 'spinster' still testifies to its having been the ordinary employment of the English young woman. It was the labour assigned to the ejected nuns by the rough earl who said, 'Go spin, ye jades, go spin.' It was the employment at which Roman matrons and Grecian princesses presided amongst their handmaids. Heathen mythology celebrated it in the three Fates spinning and measuring out the thread of human life. Holy Scripture honours it in those 'wise-hearted women' who 'did spin with their hands, and brought that which they had spun' for the construction of the Tabernacle in the wilderness: and an old English proverb carries it still farther back to the time 'when Adam delved and Eve span.' But, at last, this time-honoured domestic manufacture is quite extinct amongst us—crushed by the power of steam, overborne by a countless host of spinning jennies, and I can only just remember some of its last struggles for existence in the Steventon cottages.

Chapter III

Early Compositions—Friends at Ashe—A very old Letter—
Lines on the Death of Mrs. Lefroy—Observations on Jane
Austen's Letter-writing—Letters.

I KNOW LITTLE OF JANE Austen's childhood. Her mother followed a custom, not unusual in those days, though it seems strange to us, of putting out her babies to be nursed in a cottage in the village. The infant was daily visited by one or both of its parents, and frequently brought to them at the parsonage, but the cottage was its home, and must have remained so till it was old enough to run about and talk; for I know that one of them, in after life, used to speak of his foster mother as 'Movie,' the name by which he had called her in his infancy. It may be that the contrast between the parsonage house and the best class of cottages was not quite so extreme then as it would be now, that the one was somewhat less luxurious, and the other less squalid. It would certainly seem from the results that it was a wholesome and invigorating system, for the children were all strong and healthy. Jane was probably treated like the rest in this respect. In childhood every available opportunity of instruction was made use of. According to the ideas of the time, she was well educated, though not highly accomplished, and she certainly enjoyed that important element of mental training, associating at home with persons of cultivated intellect. It cannot be doubted that her early years were bright and happy, living, as she did, with indulgent parents, in a cheerful home, not without agreeable variety of society. To these sources of enjoyment must be added the first stirrings of talent within her, and the absorbing interest of original composition. It is impossible to say at how early an age she began to write. There are copy books extant containing tales some of which must have been composed while she was a young girl, as they had amounted to a considerable number by the time she was sixteen. Her earliest stories are of a slight and flimsy texture, and are generally intended to be nonsensical, but the nonsense has much spirit in it. They are usually preceded by a dedication of mock solemnity to some one of her family. It would seem that the grandiloquent dedications prevalent in those days had not escaped her youthful penetration. Perhaps the most characteristic feature in these early productions is that, however puerile the matter, they are always composed in pure simple English, quite free from the over-ornamented style which might be expected from so young a writer. One of her juvenile effusions is given, as a specimen of the kind of transitory amusement which Jane was continually supplying to the family party.

THE MYSTERY.
AN UNFINISHED COMEDY.

—

DEDICATION.

To the Rev. GEORGE AUSTEN.

Sir,—I humbly solicit your patronage to the following Comedy, which, though an unfinished one, is, I flatter myself, as complete a *Mystery* as any of its kind.

I am, Sir, your most humble Servant,

THE AUTHOR.

THE MYSTERY, A COMEDY.

Dramatis Personæ.

Men.	*Women.*
Col. ELLIOTT	FANNY ELLIOTT
OLD HUMBUG	Mrs. HUMBUG
YOUNG HUMBUG	*and*
Sir EDWARD SPANGLE	DAPHNE.
and	
CORYDON.	

ACT I.
Scene I.—*A Garden.*

Enter CORYDON.

Corydon. But hush: I am interrupted. [*Exit* CORYDON.

Enter OLD HUMBUG *and his* SON, *talking.*

Old Hum. It is for that reason that I wish you to follow my advice. Are you convinced of its propriety?

Young Hum. I am, sir, and will certainly act in the manner you have pointed out to me.

Old Hum. Then let us return to the house. [*Exeunt.*

Scene II.—*A parlour in* HUMBUG'S *house.*
Mrs. HUMBUG *and* FANNY *discovered at work.*

Mrs. Hum. You understand me, my love?

Fanny. Perfectly, ma'am: pray continue your narration.

Mrs. Hum. Alas! it is nearly concluded; for I have nothing more to say on the subject.

Fanny. Ah! here is Daphne.

Enter DAPHNE.

Daphne. My dear Mrs. Humbug, how d'ye do? Oh! Fanny, it is all over.

Fanny. Is it indeed!

Mrs. Hum. I'm very sorry to hear it.

Fanny. Then 'twas to no purpose that I—

Daphne. None upon earth.

Mrs. Hum. And what is to become of—?

Daphne. Oh! 'tis all settled. (*Whispers* Mrs. HUMBUG.)

Fanny. And how is it determined?

Daphne. I'll tell you. (*Whispers* FANNY.)

Mrs. Hum. And is he to—?

Daphne. I'll tell you all I know of the matter. (*Whispers* Mrs. HUMBUG *and* FANNY.)

Fanny. Well, now I know everything about it, I'll go away.

Mrs. Hum. and *Daphne.* And so will I. [*Exeunt.*

Scene III.—*The curtain rises, and discovers* Sir EDWARD SPANGLE *reclined in an elegant attitude on a sofa fast asleep.*

Enter Col. ELLIOTT.

Col. E. My daughter is not here, I see. There lies Sir Edward. Shall I tell him the secret? No, he'll certainly blab it. But he's asleep, and won't hear me;—so I'll e'en venture. (*Goes up to* Sir EDWARD, *whispers him, and exit.*)

END OF THE FIRST ACT.
FINIS.

Her own mature opinion of the desirableness of such an early habit of composition is given in the following words of a niece:—

'As I grew older, my aunt would talk to me more seriously of my reading and my amusements. I had taken early to writing verses and stories, and I am sorry to think how I troubled her with reading them. She was very kind about it, and always had some praise to bestow, but at last she warned me against spending too much time upon them. She said—how well I recollect it!—that she knew writing stories was a great amusement, and *she* thought a harmless one, though many people, she was aware, thought otherwise; but that at my age it would be bad for me to be much taken up with my own compositions. Later still—it was after she had gone to Winchester—she sent me a message to this effect, that if I would take her advice I should cease writing till I was sixteen; that she had herself often wished she had read more, and written less in the corresponding years of her own life.' As this niece was only twelve years old at the time of her aunt's death, these words seem to imply that the juvenile tales to which I have referred had, some of them at least, been written in her childhood.

But between these childish effusions, and the composition of her living works, there intervened another stage of her progress, during which she produced some stories, not without merit, but which she never considered worthy of publication. During this preparatory period her mind seems to have been working in a very different direction from that into which it ultimately settled. Instead of presenting faithful copies of nature, these tales were generally burlesques, ridiculing the improbable events and exaggerated sentiments which she had met with in sundry silly romances. Something of this fancy is to be found in *Northanger Abbey*, but she soon left it far behind in her subsequent course. It would seem as if she were first taking note of all the faults to be avoided, and curiously considering how she ought *not* to write before she attempted to put forth her strength in the right direction. The family have, rightly, I think, declined to let these early works be published. Mr. Shortreed observed very pithily of Walter Scott's early rambles on the borders, 'He was makin' himsell a' the time; but he didna ken, may be, what he was about till years had passed. At first he thought of little, I dare say, but the queerness and the fun.' And so, in a humbler way, Jane Austen was 'makin' hersell,' little thinking of future fame, but caring only for 'the queerness and the fun;' and it would be as unfair to expose this preliminary process to the world, as it would be to display all that goes on behind the curtain of the theatre before it is drawn up.

It was, however, at Steventon that the real foundations of her fame were laid. There some of her most successful writing was composed at such an early age as to make it surprising that so young a woman could have acquired the insight into character, and the nice observation of manners which they display. *Pride and Prejudice*, which some consider the most brilliant of her novels, was the first finished, if not the first begun. She began it in October 1796, before she was twenty-one years old, and completed it in about ten months, in August 1797. The title then intended for it was *First Impressions. Sense and Sensibility* was begun, in its present form, immediately after the completion of the former, in November 1797 but something similar in story and character had been written earlier under the title of *Elinor and Marianne*; and if, as is probable, a good deal of this earlier production was retained, it must form the earliest specimen of her writing that has been given to the world. *Northanger Abbey*, though not prepared for the press till 1803, was certainly first composed in 1798.

Amongst the most valuable neighbours of the Austens were Mr. and Mrs. Lefroy and their family. He was rector of the adjoining parish of Ashe; she was sister to Sir Egerton Brydges, to whom we are indebted for the earliest notice of Jane Austen that exists. In his autobiography, speaking of his visits at Ashe, he writes thus: 'The nearest neighbours of the Lefroys were the Austens of Steventon. I remember Jane Austen, the novelist, as a little child. She was very intimate with Mrs. Lefroy, and much encouraged by her. Her mother was a Miss Leigh, whose paternal grandmother was sister to the first Duke of Chandos. Mr. Austen was of a Kentish family, of which several branches have been settled in the Weald of Kent, and some are still remaining there. When I knew Jane Austen, I never suspected that she was an authoress; but my eyes told me that she was fair and handsome, slight and elegant, but with cheeks a little too full.' One may wish that Sir Egerton had dwelt rather longer on the subject of these memoirs, instead of being drawn away by his extreme love for genealogies to her great-grandmother and ancestors. That great-grandmother however lives in the family records as Mary Brydges, a daughter of Lord Chandos, married in Westminster Abbey to Theophilus Leigh of Addlestrop in 1698. When a girl she had received a curious letter of advice and reproof, written by her mother from Constantinople. Mary, or 'Poll,' was remaining in England with her grandmother, Lady Bernard, who seems to have been wealthy and inclined to be too indulgent to her granddaughter. This letter is given. Any such authentic document, two hundred years old, dealing with domestic details, must possess some interest. This is remarkable, not only as a specimen of the homely language in which ladies of rank then expressed themselves, but from the sound sense which it contains. Forms of expression vary, but good sense and right principles are the same in the nineteenth that they were in the seventeenth century.

'My deares Poll,

'Y^r letters by Cousin Robbert Serle arrived here not before the 27th of Aprill, yett were they hartily wellcome to us, bringing ye joyful news which a great while we had longed for of my most dear Mother & all other relations & friends good health which I beseech God continue to you all, & as I observe in y^{rs} to y^r Sister Betty ye extraordinary kindness of (as I may truly say) the best Moth^r & Gnd Moth^r in the world in pinching herself to make you fine, so I cannot but admire her great good Housewifry in affording you so very plentifull an allowance, & yett to increase her Stock at the rate I find she hath done; & think I can never sufficiently mind you how very much it is y^r duty on all occasions to pay her y^r gratitude in all humble submission & obedience to all her commands soe long as you live. I must tell you 'tis to her bounty & care in ye greatest measure you are like to owe y^r well living in this world, & as you cannot but be very sensible you are an extra-ordinary charge to her so it behoves you to take particular heed th^t in ye whole course of y^r life, you render her a proportionable comfort, especially since 'tis ye best way you can ever hope to make her such amends as God requires of y^r hands. but Poll! it grieves me a little y^t I am forced to take notice of & reprove you for some vaine expressions in y^r lettrs to y^r Sister—you say concerning y^r allowance "you aime to bring y^r bread & cheese even" in this I do not discommend you, for a foule shame indeed it would be should you out run the Constable having soe liberall a provision made you for y^r maintenance—but ye reason you give for y^r resolution I cannot at all approve for you say "to spend more you can't" thats because you have it not to spend, otherwise it seems you would. So y^t 'tis y^r Grandmoth^{rs} discretion & not yours th^t keeps you from extravagancy, which plainly appears in ye close of y^r sentence, saying y^t you think it simple covetousness to save out of y^{rs} but 'tis my opinion if you lay all on y^r back 'tis ten tymes a greater sin & shame th^n to save some what out of soe large an allowance in y^r purse to help you at a dead lift. Child, we all know our beginning, but who knows his end? Y^e best use th^t can be made of fair weath^r is to provide against foule & 'tis great discretion & of noe small commendations for a young woman betymes to shew herself housewifly & frugal. Y^r Mother neither Maide nor wife ever yett bestowed forty pounds a yeare on herself & yett if you never fall und^r a worse reputation in ye world th^n she (I thank God for it) hath hitherto done, you need not repine at it, & you cannot be ignorant of ye difference th^t was between my fortune & what you are to expect. You ought likewise to consider th^t you have seven brothers & sisters & you are all one man's children & therefore it is very unreasonable that one should expect to be preferred in finery soe much above all ye rest for 'tis impossible you should soe much mistake y^r ffather's condition as to fancy he is able to allow every one of you forty pounds a yeare a piece, for such an allowance with the charge of their diett over and above will amount to at least five hundred pounds a yeare, a sum y^r poor ffather can ill spare, besides doe but bethink y^{r}self what a ridiculous sight it will be when y^r grandmoth^r & you come to us to have noe less th^n seven waiting gentlewomen in one house, for what reason can you give why every one of y^r Sist^{rs} should not have every one of y^m a Maide as well as you, & though you may spare to pay y^r maide's wages out of y^r allowance yett you take no care of ye unnecessary charge you put y^r ffath^r to in y^r increase of his family, whereas if it were not a piece of pride to have ye name of keeping y^r maide she y^t waits on y^r good Grandmother might easily doe as formerly you know she hath done, all ye business you have for a maide unless as you grow old^r you grow a veryer Foole which God forbid!

'Poll, you live in a place where you see great plenty & splendour but let not ye allurements of earthly pleasures tempt you to forget or neglect ye duty of a good Christian in dressing y^r bett^r part which is y^r soule, as will best please God. I am not against y^r going decent & neate as becomes y^r ffathers daughter but to clothe y^{r}self rich & be running into every gaudy fashion can never become y^r circumstances & instead of doing you creditt & getting you a good prefer^{nt} it is ye readiest way you can take to fright all sober men from ever thinking of matching th^{m}selves with women that live above thy^r fortune, & if this be a wise way of spending money judge you! & besides, doe but reflect what an od sight it will be to a stranger that comes to our house to see y^r Grandmoth^r y^r Moth^r & all y^r Sisters in a plane dress & you only trick^d

up like a bartlemew-babby—you know what sort of people those are th^t can't faire well but they must cry rost meate now what effect could you imagine y^r writing in such a high straine to y^r Sisters could have but eithe^r to provoke th^m to envy you or murmur against us. I must tell you neith^r of y^r Sisters have ever had twenty pounds a yeare allowance from us yett, & yett they^r dress hath not disparaged neith^r th^m nor us & without incurring ye censure of simple covetousness they will have some what to shew out of their saving that will doe th^m creditt & I expect y^t you th^t are they^r elder Sister sh^d rather sett th^m examples of ye like nature th^n tempt th^m from treading in ye steps of their good Grandmoth^r & poor Moth^r. This is not half what might be saide on this occasion but believing thee to be a very good natured dutyfull child I sh^d have thought it a great deal too much but y^t having in my coming hither past through many most desperate dangers I cannot forbear thinking & preparing myself for all events, & therefore not knowing how it may please God to dispose of us I conclude it my duty to God & thee my d^r child to lay this matter as home to thee as I could, assuring you my daily prayers are not nor shall not be wanting that God may give you grace always to remember to make a right use of this truly affectionate counsell of y^r poor Moth^r. & though I speak very plaine down-right english to you yett I would not have you doubt but that I love you as hartily as any child I have & if you serve God and take good courses I promise you my kindness to you shall be according to y^r own hart's desire, for you may be certain I can aime at nothing in what I have now writ but y^r real good which to promote shall be ye study & care day & night

'Of my dear Poll
'thy truly affectionate Mothr.
'Eliza Chandos.

'Pera of Galata, May ye 6th 1686.

'P.S.—Thy ffath^r & I send thee our blessing, & all thy broth^{rs} & sist^{rs} theyr service. Our harty & affectionate service to my broth^r & sist^r Childe & all my dear cozens. When you see my Lady Worster & cozen Howlands pray present th^m my most humble service.'

This letter shows that the wealth acquired by trade was already manifesting itself in contrast with the straitened circumstances of some of the nobility. Mary Brydges's 'poor ffather,' in whose household economy was necessary, was the King of England's ambassador at Constantinople; the grandmother, who lived in 'great plenty and splendour,' was the widow of a Turkey merchant. But then, as now, it would seem, rank had the power of attracting and absorbing wealth.

At Ashe also Jane became acquainted with a member of the Lefroy family, who was still living when I began these memoirs, a few months ago; the Right Hon. Thomas Lefroy, late Chief Justice of Ireland. One must look back more than seventy years to reach the time when these two bright young persons were, for a short time, intimately acquainted with each other, and then separated on their several courses, never to meet again; both destined to attain some distinction in their different ways, one to survive the other for more than half a century, yet in his extreme old age to remember and speak, as he sometimes did, of his former companion, as one to be much admired, and not easily forgotten by those who had ever known her.

Mrs. Lefroy herself was a remarkable person. Her rare endowments of goodness, talents, graceful person, and engaging manners, were sufficient to secure her a prominent place in any society into which she was thrown; while her enthusiastic eagerness of disposition rendered her especially attractive to a clever and lively girl. She was killed by a fall from her horse on Jane's birthday, Dec. 16, 1804. The following lines to her memory were written by Jane four years afterwards, when she was thirty-three years old. They are given, not for their merits as poetry, but to show how deep and lasting was the impression made by the elder friend on the mind of the younger:—

To the Memory of Mrs. Lefroy.

1.

The day returns again, my natal day;
   What mix'd emotions in my mind arise!
Beloved Friend; four years have passed away
   Since thou wert snatched for ever from our eyes.

2.

The day commemorative of my birth,
   Bestowing life, and light, and hope to me,

Brings back the hour which was thy last on earth.
  O! bitter pang of torturing memory!

3.
Angelic woman! past my power to praise
  In language meet thy talents, temper, mind,
Thy solid worth, thy captivating grace,
  Thou friend and ornament of human kind.

4.
But come, fond Fancy, thou indulgent power;
  Hope is desponding, chill, severe, to thee:
Bless thou this little portion of an hour;
  Let me behold her as she used to be.

5.
I see her here with all her smiles benign,
  Her looks of eager love, her accents sweet,
That voice and countenance almost divine,
  Expression, harmony, alike complete.

6.
Listen! It is not sound alone, 'tis sense,
  'Tis genius, taste, and tenderness of soul:
'Tis genuine warmth of heart without pretence,
  And purity of mind that crowns the whole.

7.
She speaks! 'Tis eloquence, that grace of tongue,
  So rare, so lovely, never misapplied
By her, to palliate vice, or deck a wrong:
  She speaks and argues but on virtue's side.

8.
Hers is the energy of soul sincere;
  Her Christian spirit, ignorant to feign,
Seeks but to comfort, heal, enlighten, cheer,
  Confer a pleasure or prevent a pain.

9.
Can aught enhance such goodness? yes, to me
  Her partial favour from my earliest years
Consummates all: ah! give me but to see
  Her smile of love! The vision disappears.

10.
'Tis past and gone. We meet no more below,
    Short is the cheat of Fancy o'er the tomb.
Oh! might I hope to equal bliss to go,
    To meet thee, angel, in thy future home.

11.
Fain would I feel an union with thy fate:
    Fain would I seek to draw an omen fair
From this connection in our earthly date.
    Indulge the harmless weakness. Reason, spare.

The loss of their first home is generally a great grief to young persons of strong feeling and lively imagination; and Jane was exceedingly unhappy when she was told that her father, now seventy years of age, had determined to resign his duties to his eldest son, who was to be his successor in the Rectory of Steventon, and to remove with his wife and daughters to Bath. Jane had been absent from home when this resolution was taken; and, as her father was always rapid both in forming his resolutions and in acting on them, she had little time to reconcile herself to the change.

❦

A wish has sometimes been expressed that some of Jane Austen's letters should be published. Some entire letters, and many extracts, will be given in this memoir; but the reader must be warned not to expect too much from them. With regard to accuracy of language indeed every word of them might be printed without correction. The style is always clear, and generally animated, while a vein of humour continually gleams through the whole; but the materials may be thought inferior to the execution, for they treat only of the details of domestic life. There is in them no notice of politics or public events; scarcely any discussions on literature, or other subjects of general interest. They may be said to resemble the nest which some little bird builds of the materials nearest at hand, of the twigs and mosses supplied by the tree in which it is placed; curiously constructed out of the simplest matters.

Her letters have very seldom the date of the year, or the signature of her Christian name at full length; but it has been easy to ascertain their dates, either from the post-mark, or from their contents.

The two following letters are the earliest that I have seen. They were both written in November 1800; before the family removed from Steventon. Some of the same circumstances are referred to in both.

The first is to her sister Cassandra, who was then staying with their brother Edward at Godmersham Park, Kent:—

'Steventon, Saturday evening, Nov. 8th.

'My dear Cassandra,

'I thank you for so speedy a return to my two last, and particularly thank you for your anecdote of Charlotte Graham and her cousin, Harriet Bailey, which has very much amused both my mother and myself. If you can learn anything farther of that interesting affair, I hope you will mention it. I have two messages; let me get rid of them, and then my paper will be my own. Mary fully intended writing to you by Mr. Chute's frank, and only happened entirely to forget it, but will write soon; and my father wishes Edward to send him a memorandum of the price of the hops. The tables are come, and give general contentment. I had not expected that they would so perfectly suit the fancy of us all three, or that we should so well agree in the disposition of them; but nothing except their own surface can have been smoother. The two ends put together form one constant table for everything, and the centre piece stands exceedingly well under the glass, and holds a great deal most commodiously, without looking awkwardly. They are both covered with green baize, and send their best love. The Pembroke has got its destination by the sideboard, and my mother has great delight in keeping her money and papers locked up. The little table which used to stand there has most conveniently taken itself off into the best bedroom; and we are now in want only of the chiffonniere, which is neither finished nor come. So much for that subject; I now come to another, of a very different nature, as other subjects are very apt to be. Earle Harwood has been again giving uneasiness to his family and talk to the neighbourhood; in the present instance, however, he is only unfortunate, and not in fault.

'About ten days ago, in cocking a pistol in the guard-room at Marcau, he accidentally shot himself through the thigh. Two young Scotch surgeons in the island were polite enough to propose taking off the thigh at once, but to that he would not consent; and accordingly in his wounded state was put on board a cutter and conveyed to Haslar Hospital, at Gosport, where the bullet was extracted, and where he now is, I hope, in a fair way of doing well. The surgeon of the hospital wrote to the family on the occasion, and John Harwood went down to him immediately, attended by James,[21] whose object in going was to be the means of bringing back the earliest intelligence to Mr. and Mrs. Harwood, whose anxious sufferings, particularly those of the latter, have of course been dreadful. They went down on Tuesday, and James came back the next day, bringing such favourable accounts as greatly to lessen the distress of the family at Deane, though it will probably be a long while before Mrs. Harwood can be quite at ease. *One* most material comfort, however, they have; the assurance of its being really an accidental wound, which is not only positively declared by Earle himself, but is likewise testified by the particular direction of the bullet. Such a wound could not have been received in a duel. At present he is going on very well, but the surgeon will not declare him to be in no danger.[22] Mr. Heathcote met with a genteel little accident the other day in hunting. He got off to lead his horse over a hedge, or a house, or something, and his horse in his haste trod upon his leg, or rather ancle, I believe, and it is not certain whether the small bone is not broke. Martha has accepted Mary's invitation for Lord Portsmouth's ball. He has not yet sent out his own invitations, but *that* does not signify; Martha comes, and a ball there is to be. I think it will be too early in her mother's absence for me to return with her.

'*Sunday Evening.*—We have had a dreadful storm of wind in the fore part of this day, which has done a great deal of mischief among our trees. I was sitting alone in the dining-room when an odd kind of crash startled me—in a moment afterwards it was repeated. I then went to the window, which I reached just in time to see the last of our two highly valued elms descend into the Sweep!!!! The other, which had fallen, I suppose, in the first crash, and which was the nearest to the pond, taking a more easterly direction, sunk among our screen of chestnuts and firs, knocking down one spruce-fir, beating off the head of another, and stripping the two corner chestnuts of several branches in its fall. This is

---

21 James, the writer's eldest brother.
22 The limb was saved.

not all. One large elm out of the two on the left-hand side as you enter what I call the elm walk, was likewise blown down; the maple bearing the weathercock was broke in two, and what I regret more than all the rest is, that all the three elms which grew in Hall's meadow, and gave such ornament to it, are gone; two were blown down, and the other so much injured that it cannot stand. I am happy to add, however, that no greater evil than the loss of trees has been the consequence of the storm in this place, or in our immediate neighbourhood. We grieve, therefore, in some comfort.

'I am yours ever,

'J.A.'

The next letter, written four days later than the former, was addressed to Miss Lloyd, an intimate friend, whose sister (my mother) was married to Jane's eldest brother:—

'Steventon, Wednesday evening, Nov. 12th.

'My dear Martha,

'I did not receive your note yesterday till after Charlotte had left Deane, or I would have sent my answer by her, instead of being the means, as I now must be, of lessening the elegance of your new dress for the Hurstbourne ball by the value of 3d.[23] You are very good in wishing to see me at Ibthorp so soon, and I am equally good in wishing to come to you. I believe our merit in that respect is much upon a par, our self-denial mutually strong. Having paid this tribute of praise to the virtue of both, I shall here have done with panegyric, and proceed to plain matter of fact. In about a fortnight's time I hope to be with you. I have two reasons for not being able to come before. I wish so to arrange my visit as to spend some days with you after your mother's return. In the 1st place, that I may have the pleasure of seeing her, and in the 2nd, that I may have a better chance of bringing you back with me. Your promise in my favour was not quite absolute, but if your will is not perverse, you and I will do all in our power to overcome your scruples of conscience. I hope we shall meet next week to talk all this over, till we have tired ourselves with the very idea of my visit before my visit

23 [Three pence: at the time the pound was divided into 240 pennies.]

begins. Our invitations for the 19th are arrived, and very curiously are they worded.[24] Mary mentioned to you yesterday poor Earle's unfortunate accident, I dare say. He does not seem to be going on very well. The two or three last posts have brought less and less favourable accounts of him. John Harwood has gone to Gosport again to-day. We have two families of friends now who are in a most anxious state; for though by a note from Catherine this morning there seems now to be a revival of hope at Manydown, its continuance may be too reasonably doubted. Mr. Heathcote,[25] however, who has broken the small bone of his leg, is so good as to be going on very well. It would be really too much to have three people to care for.

'You distress me cruelly by your request about books. I cannot think of any to bring with me, nor have I any idea of our wanting them. I come to you to be talked to, not to read or hear reading; I can do that at home; and indeed I am now laying in a stock of intelligence to pour out on you as my share of the conversation. I am reading Henry's History of England, which I will repeat to you in any manner you may prefer, either in a loose, desultory, unconnected stream, or dividing my recital, as the historian divides it himself, into seven parts:—The Civil and Military: Religion: Constitution: Learning and Learned Men: Arts and Sciences: Commerce, Coins, and Shipping: and Manners. So that for every evening in the week there will be a different subject. The Friday's lot—Commerce, Coins, and Shipping—you will find the least entertaining; but the next evening's portion will make amends. With such a provision on my part, if you will do yours by repeating the French Grammar, and Mrs. Stent[26] will now and then ejaculate some wonder about the cocks and hens, what can we want? Farewell for a short time. We all unite in best love, and I am your very affectionate

'J.A.'

---

24 The invitation, the ball dress, and some other things in this and the preceding letter refer to a ball annually given at Hurstbourne Park, on the anniversary of the Earl of Portsmouth's marriage with his first wife. He was the Lord Portsmouth whose eccentricities afterwards became notorious, and the invitations, as well as other arrangements about these balls, were of a peculiar character.

25 The father of Sir William Heathcote, of Hursley, who was married to a daughter of Mr. Bigg Wither, of Manydown, and lived in the neighbourhood.

26 A very dull old lady, then residing with Mrs. Lloyd.

The two next letters must have been written early in 1801, after the removal from Steventon had been decided on, but before it had taken place. They refer to the two brothers who were at sea, and give some idea of a kind of anxieties and uncertainties to which sisters are seldom subject in these days of peace, steamers, and electric telegraphs. At that time ships were often windbound or becalmed, or driven wide of their destination; and sometimes they had orders to alter their course for some secret service; not to mention the chance of conflict with a vessel of superior power—no improbable occurrence before the battle of Trafalgar. Information about relatives on board men-of-war was scarce and scanty, and often picked up by hearsay or chance means; and every scrap of intelligence was proportionably valuable:—

'My dear Cassandra,

'I should not have thought it necessary to write to you so soon, but for the arrival of a letter from Charles to myself. It was written last Saturday from off the Start, and conveyed to Popham Lane by Captain Boyle, on his way to Midgham. He came from Lisbon in the *Endymion*.[27] I will copy Charles's account of his conjectures about Frank: "He has not seen my brother lately, nor does he expect to find him arrived, as he met Captain Inglis at Rhodes, going up to take command of the *Petrel*, as he was coming down; but supposes he will arrive in less than a fortnight from this time, in some ship which is expected to reach England about that time with dispatches from Sir Ralph Abercrombie." The event must show what sort of a conjuror Captain Boyle is. The *Endymion* has not been plagued with any more prizes.[28] Charles spent three pleasant days in Lisbon.

'They were very well satisfied with their royal passenger,[29] whom they found jolly and affable, who talks of Lady Augusta as his wife, and seems much attached to her.

---

27 [HMS *Endymion* was a 40-gun Royal Navy frigate that saw action in many wars. It was launched in 1797 and broken up in 1868.]
28 [In order to encourage ships' crews, the government paid a bounty to Royal Navy personnel for the sinking or capturing of enemy vessels. The practice was phased out in 1918.]
29 The Duke of Sussex, son of George III, married, without royal consent, to the Lady Augusta Murray.

'When this letter was written, the *Endymion* was becalmed, but Charles hoped to reach Portsmouth by Monday or Tuesday. He received my letter, communicating our plans, before he left England; was much surprised, of course, but is quite reconciled to them, and means to come to Steventon once more while Steventon is ours.'

From a letter written later in the same year:—

'Charles has received £30 for his share of the privateer, and expects £10 more; but of what avail is it to take prizes if he lays out the produce in presents to his sisters? He has been buying gold chains and topaze crosses for us. He must be well scolded. The *Endymion* has already received orders for taking troops to Egypt, which I should not like at all if I did not trust to Charles being removed from her somehow or other before she sails. He knows nothing of his own destination, he says, but desires me to write directly, as the *Endymion* will probably sail in three or four days. He will receive my yesterday's letter, and I shall write again by this post to thank and reproach him. We shall be unbearably fine.'

Chapter IV

Removal from Steventon—Residences at Bath and at Southampton—Settling at Chawton.

THE FAMILY REMOVED TO Bath in the spring of 1801, where they resided first at No. 4 Sydney Terrace, and afterwards in Green Park Buildings. I do not know whether they were at all attracted to Bath by the circumstance that Mrs. Austen's only brother, Mr. Leigh Perrot, spent part of every year there. The name of Perrot, together with a small estate at Northleigh in Oxfordshire, had been bequeathed to him by a great uncle. I must devote a few sentences to this very old and now extinct branch of the Perrot family; for one of the last survivors, Jane Perrot, married to a Walker, was Jane Austen's great grandmother, from whom she derived her Christian name. The Perrots were settled in Pembrokeshire at least as early as the thirteenth century. They were probably some of the settlers whom the policy of our Plantagenet kings placed in that county, which thence acquired the name of 'England beyond Wales,' for the double purpose of keeping open a communication with Ireland from Milford Haven, and of overawing the Welsh. One of the family seems to have carried out this latter purpose very vigorously; for it is recorded of him that he slew *twenty-six men* of Kemaes, a district of Wales, and *one wolf.* The manner in which the two kinds of game are classed together, and the disproportion of numbers, are remarkable; but probably at that time the wolves had been so closely killed down, that *lupicide* was become a more rare and distinguished exploit than *homicide.* The last of this family died about 1778, and their property was divided between Leighs and Musgraves, the larger portion going to the latter. Mr. Leigh Perrot pulled down the mansion, and sold the estate to the Duke of Marlborough, and the name of these Perrots is now to be found only on some monuments in the church of Northleigh.

Mr. Leigh Perrot was also one of several cousins to whom a life interest in the Stoneleigh property in Warwickshire was left, after the extinction of the earlier Leigh peerage, but he compromised his claim to the succession in his lifetime. He married a niece of Sir Montague Cholmeley of Lincolnshire. He was a man of considerable natural power, with much of the wit of his uncle, the Master of Balliol, and wrote clever epigrams and riddles, some of which, though without his name, found their way into print; but he lived a very retired life, dividing his time between Bath and his place in Berkshire called Scarlets. Jane's letters from Bath make frequent mention of this uncle and aunt.

The unfinished story, now published under the title of *The Watsons*, must have been written during the author's residence in Bath. In the autumn of 1804 she spent some weeks at Lyme, and became acquainted with the Cobb, which she afterwards made memorable for the fall of Louisa Musgrove. In February 1805, her father died at Bath, and was buried at Walcot Church. The widow and daughters went into lodgings for a few months, and then removed to Southampton. The only records that I can find about her during those four years are the three following letters to her sister; one from Lyme, the others from Bath. They shew that she went a good deal into society, in a quiet way, chiefly with ladies; and that her eyes were always open to minute traits of character in those with whom she associated:—

Extract from a letter from Jane Austen to her Sister.

'Lyme, Friday, Sept. 14 (1804).

'My dear Cassandra,—I take the first sheet of fine striped paper to thank you for your letter from Weymouth, and express my hopes of your being at Ibthorp before this time. I expect to hear that you reached it yesterday evening, being able to get as far as Blandford on Wednesday. Your account of Weymouth contains nothing which strikes me so forcibly as there being no ice in the town. For every other vexation I was in some measure prepared, and particularly for your disappointment in not seeing the Royal Family go on board on Tuesday, having already heard from Mr. Crawford that he had seen you in the very act of being too late. But for there being no ice, what could prepare me! You found my letter at Andover, I hope, yesterday, and have now for many hours been satisfied that your kind anxiety on my behalf was as much thrown away as kind anxiety usually is. I continue quite well; in proof of which I have bathed again this morning. It was absolutely necessary that I should have the little fever and indisposition which I had: it has been all the fashion this week in Lyme. We are quite settled in our lodgings by this time, as you may suppose, and everything goes on in the usual order. The servants behave very well, and make no difficulties, though nothing certainly can exceed the inconvenience of the offices, except the general dirtiness of the house and furniture, and all its inhabitants. I endeavour, as far as I can, to supply your place, and be useful, and keep things in order. I detect dirt in the water decanters, as fast as I can, and keep everything as it was under your administration ... The ball last night was pleasant, but not full for Thursday. My father staid contentedly till half-past nine (we went a little after eight), and then walked home with James and a lanthorn, though I believe the lanthorn was not lit, as the moon was up; but sometimes this lanthorn may be a great convenience to him. My mother and I staid about an hour later. Nobody asked me the two first dances; the two next I danced with Mr. Crawford, and had I chosen to stay longer might have danced with Mr. Granville, Mrs. Granville's son, whom my dear friend Miss A. introduced to me, or with a new odd-looking man who had been eyeing me for some time, and at last, without any introduction, asked me if I meant to dance again. I think he must be Irish by his ease, and because I imagine him to belong to the hon^{bl} B.'s, who are son, and son's wife of an Irish viscount, bold queer-looking people, just fit to be quality at Lyme. I called yesterday morning (ought it not in strict propriety to be termed yester-morning?) on Miss A. and was introduced to her father and mother. Like other young ladies she is considerably genteeler than her parents. Mrs. A. sat darning a pair of stockings the whole of my visit. But do not mention this at home, lest a warning should act as an example. We afterwards walked together for an hour on the Cobb; she is very converseable in a common way; I do not perceive wit or genius, but she has sense and some degree of taste, and her manners are very engaging. She seems to like people rather too easily.

'Yours affect^{ly},

'J.A.'

Letter from Jane Austen to her sister Cassandra at Ibthorp, alluding to the sudden death of Mrs. Lloyd at that place:—

'25 Gay Street (Bath), Monday, April 8, 1805.

'My dear Cassandra,—Here is a day for you. Did Bath or Ibthorp ever see such an 8th of April? It is March and April together; the glare of the one and the warmth of the other. We do nothing but walk about. As far as your means will admit, I hope you profit by such weather too.

I dare say you are already the better for change of place. We were out again last night. Miss Irvine invited us, when I met her in the Crescent, to drink tea with them, but I rather declined it, having no idea that my mother would be disposed for another evening visit there so soon; but when I gave her the message, I found her very well inclined to go; and accordingly, on leaving Chapel, we walked to Lansdown. This morning we have been to see Miss Chamberlaine look hot on horseback. Seven years and four months ago we went to the same riding-house to see Miss Lefroy's performance![30] What a different set are we now moving in! But seven years, I suppose, are enough to change every pore of one's skin and every feeling of one's mind. We did not walk long in the Crescent yesterday. It was hot and not crowded enough; so we went into the field, and passed close by S.T. and Miss S.[31] again. I have not yet seen her face, but neither her dress nor air have anything of the dash or stylishness which the Browns talked of; quite the contrary; indeed, her dress is not even smart, and her appearance very quiet. Miss Irvine says she is never speaking a word. Poor wretch; I am afraid she is *en péni-tence*.[32] Here has been that excellent Mrs. Coulthart calling, while my mother was out, and I was believed to be so. I always respected her, as a good-hearted friendly woman. And the Browns have been here; I find their affidavits on the table. The "Ambuscade" reached Gibraltar on the 9th of March, and found all well; so say the papers. We have had no letters from anybody, but we expect to hear from Edward to-morrow, and from you soon afterwards. How happy they are at Godmersham now! I shall be very glad of a letter from Ibthorp, that I may know how you all are, but particularly yourself. This is nice weather for Mrs. J. Austen's going to Speen, and I hope she will have a pleasant visit there. I expect a prodigious account of the christening dinner; perhaps it brought you at last into the company of Miss Dundas again.

'*Tuesday.*—I received your letter last night, and wish it may be soon followed by another to say that all is over; but I cannot help thinking that nature will struggle again, and produce a revival. Poor woman!

---

30 Here is evidence that Jane Austen was acquainted with Bath before it became her residence in 1801.

31 A gentleman and lady lately engaged to be married.

32 ['In penitence': the French expression *mettre un enfant en pénitence* means to make a child stand in the corner.]

May her end be peaceful and easy as the exit we have witnessed! And I dare say it will. If there is no revival, suffering must be all over; even the consciousness of existence, I suppose, was gone when you wrote. The nonsense I have been writing in this and in my last letter seems out of place at such a time, but I will not mind it; it will do you no harm, and nobody else will be attacked by it. I am heartily glad that you can speak so comfortably of your own health and looks, though I can scarcely comprehend the latter being really approved. Could travelling fifty miles produce such an immediate change? You were looking very poorly here, and everybody seemed sensible of it. Is there a charm in a hack postchaise? But if there were, Mrs. Craven's carriage might have undone it all. I am much obliged to you for the time and trouble you have bestowed on Mary's cap, and am glad it pleases her; but it will prove a useless gift at present, I suppose. Will not she leave Ibthorp on her mother's death? As a companion you are all that Martha can be supposed to want, and in that light, under these circumstances, your visit will indeed have been well timed.

'*Thursday.*—I was not able to go on yesterday; all my wit and leisure were bestowed on letters to Charles and Henry. To the former I wrote in consequence of my mother's having seen in the papers that the *Urania* was waiting at Portsmouth for the convoy for Halifax. This is nice, as it is only three weeks ago that you wrote by the *Camilla*. I wrote to Henry because I had a letter from him in which he desired to hear from me very soon. His to me was most affectionate and kind, as well as entertaining; there is no merit to him in *that*; he cannot help being amusing. He offers to meet us on the sea coast, if the plan of which Edward gave him some hint takes place. Will not this be making the execution of such a plan more desirable and delightful than ever? He talks of the rambles we took together last summer with pleasing affection.

'Yours ever,

'J.A.'

From the same to the same.

'Gay St. Sunday Evening,
'April 21 (1805).

My dear Cassandra,—I am much obliged to you for writing to me again so soon; your letter yesterday was quite an unexpected pleasure.

Poor Mrs. Stent! it has been her lot to be always in the way; but we must be merciful, for perhaps in time we may come to be Mrs. Stents ourselves, unequal to anything, and unwelcome to everybody ... My morning engagement was with the Cookes, and our party consisted of George and Mary, a Mr. L., Miss B., who had been with us at the concert, and the youngest Miss W. Not Julia; we have done with her; she is very ill; but Mary. Mary W.'s turn is actually come to be grown up, and have a fine complexion, and wear great square muslin shawls. I have not expressly enumerated myself among the party, but there I was, and my cousin George was very kind, and talked sense to me every now and then, in the intervals of his more animated fooleries with Miss B., who is very young, and rather handsome, and whose gracious manners, ready wit, and solid remarks, put me somewhat in mind of my old acquaintance L.L. There was a monstrous deal of stupid quizzing and common-place nonsense talked, but scarcely any wit; all that bordered on it or on sense came from my cousin George, whom altogether I like very well. Mr. B. seems nothing more than a tall young man. My evening engagement and walk was with Miss A., who had called on me the day before, and gently upbraided me in her turn with a change of manners to her since she had been in Bath, or at least of late. Unlucky me! that my notice should be of such consequence, and my manners so bad! She was so well disposed, and so reasonable, that I soon forgave her, and made this engagement with her in proof of it. She is really an agreeable girl, so I think I may like her; and her great want of a companion at home, which may well make any tolerable acquaintance important to her, gives her another claim on my attention. I shall endeavour as much as possible to keep my intimacies in their proper place, and prevent their clashing. Among so many friends, it will be well if I do not get into a scrape; and now here is Miss Blashford come. I should have gone distracted if the Bullers had staid ... When I tell you I have been visiting a countess this morning, you will immediately, with great justice, but no truth, guess it to be Lady Roden. No: it is Lady Leven, the mother of Lord Balgonie. On receiving a message from Lord and Lady Leven through the Mackays, declaring their intention of waiting on us, we thought it right to go to them. I hope we have not done too much, but the friends and admirers of Charles must be attended to. They seem very reasonable, good sort of people, very civil, and full of his praise.[33] We were shewn at first into an empty drawing-room, and presently in came his lordship, not knowing who we were, to apologise for the servant's mistake, and to say himself what was untrue, that Lady Leven was not within. He is a tall gentlemanlike looking man, with spectacles, and rather deaf. After sitting with him ten minutes we walked away; but Lady Leven coming out of the dining parlour as we passed the door, we were obliged to attend her back to it, and pay our visit over again. She is a stout woman, with a very handsome face. By this means we had the pleasure of hearing Charles's praises twice over. They think themselves excessively obliged to him, and estimate him so highly as to wish Lord Balgonie, when he is quite recovered, to go out to him. There is a pretty little Lady Marianne of the party, to be shaken hands with, and asked if she remembered Mr. Austen: ...

'I shall write to Charles by the next packet, unless you tell me in the meantime of your intending to do it.

'Believe me, if you chuse,

'Y^r aff^{te} Sister.'

Jane did not estimate too highly the 'Cousin George' mentioned in the foregoing letter; who might easily have been superior in sense and wit to the rest of the party. He was the Rev. George Leigh Cooke, long known and respected at Oxford, where he held important offices, and had the privilege of helping to form the minds of men more eminent than himself. As Tutor in Corpus Christi College, he became instructor to some of the most distinguished undergraduates of that time: amongst others to Dr. Arnold, the Rev. John Keble, and Sir John Coleridge. The latter has mentioned him in terms of affectionate regard, both in his *Memoir of Keble*, and in a letter which appears in Dean Stanley's *Life of Arnold*.[34] Mr. Cooke was also an impressive preacher of earnest awakening sermons. I remember to have heard it observed by some of my undergraduate friends that, after all, there was more good to be got from George Cooke's plain sermons than from

---

33 It seems that Charles Austen, then first lieutenant of the *Endymion*, had had an opportunity of shewing attention and kindness to some of Lord Leven's family.

34 [Arthur Stanley, 1815–81, was Dean of Westminster. The subject of the Dean's book, published in 1844, was Thomas Arnold, 1795–1842, an English educator and historian.]

much of the more laboured oratory of the University pulpit. He was frequently Examiner in the schools, and occupied the chair of the Sedleian Professor of Natural Philosophy, from 1810 to 1853.

Before the end of 1805, the little family party removed to Southampton. They resided in a commodious old-fashioned house in a corner of Castle Square.

I have no letters of my aunt, nor any other record of her, during her four years' residence at Southampton; and though I now began to know, and, what was the same thing, to love her myself, yet my observations were only those of a young boy, and were not capable of penetrating her character, or estimating her powers. I have, however, a lively recollection of some local circumstances at Southampton, and as they refer chiefly to things which have been long ago swept away, I will record them. My grandmother's house had a pleasant garden, bounded on one side by the old city walls; the top of this wall was sufficiently wide to afford a pleasant walk, with an extensive view, easily accessible to ladies by steps. This must have been a part of the identical walls which witnessed the embarkation of Henry V before the battle of Agincourt, and the detection of the conspiracy of Cambridge, Scroop, and Grey, which Shakespeare has made so picturesque; when, according to the chorus in *Henry V,* the citizens saw

> The well-appointed King at Hampton Pier
> Embark his royalty.

Among the records of the town of Southampton, they have a minute and authentic account, drawn up at that time, of the encampment of Henry V near the town, before his embarkment for France. It is remarkable that the place where the army was encamped, then a low level plain, is now entirely covered by the sea, and is called Westport.[35] At that time Castle Square was occupied by a fantastic edifice, too large for the space in which it stood, though too small to accord well with its castellated style, erected by the second Marquis of Lansdowne, half-brother to the well-known statesman, who succeeded him in the title. The Marchioness had a light phaeton, drawn by six, and sometimes by eight little ponies, each pair decreasing in size, and becoming lighter

---

35 See Wharton's note to Johnson and Steevens' *Shakespeare*. [*The Works of Shakespeare with the Corrections and Illustrations of Various Commentators* (10 vols., 1773).]

in colour, through all the grades of dark brown, light brown, bay, and chestnut, as it was placed farther away from the carriage. The two leading pairs were managed by two boyish postilions, the two pairs nearest to the carriage were driven in hand. It was a delight to me to look down from the window and see this fairy equipage put together; for the premises of this castle were so contracted that the whole process went on in the little space that remained of the open square. Like other fairy works, however, it all proved evanescent. Not only carriage and ponies, but castle itself, soon vanished away, 'like the baseless fabric of a vision.' On the death of the Marquis in 1809, the castle was pulled down. Few probably remember its existence; and any one who might visit the place now would wonder how it ever could have stood there.

In 1809 Mr. Knight was able to offer his mother the choice of two houses on his property; one near his usual residence at Godmersham Park in Kent; the other near Chawton House, his occasional residence in Hampshire. The latter was chosen; and in that year the mother and daughters, together with Miss Lloyd, a near connection who lived with them, settled themselves at Chawton Cottage.

Chawton may be called the *second*, as well as the *last* home of Jane Austen; for during the temporary residences of the party at Bath and Southampton she was only a sojourner in a strange land; but here she found a real home amongst her own people. It so happened that during her residence at Chawton circumstances brought several of her brothers and their families within easy distance of the house. Chawton must also be considered the place most closely connected with her career as a writer; for there it was that, in the maturity of her mind, she either wrote or rearranged, and prepared for publication the books by which she has become known to the world. This was the home where, after a few years, while still in the prime of life, she began to droop and wither away, and which she left only in the last stage of her illness, yielding to the persuasion of friends hoping against hope.

This house stood in the village of Chawton, about a mile from Alton, on the right hand side, just where the road to Winchester branches off from that to Gosport. It was so close to the road that the front door opened upon it; while a very narrow enclosure, paled in on each side, protected the building from danger of collision with any runaway vehicle. I believe it had been originally built for an inn, for which purpose it was certainly well situated. Afterwards it had been occupied by

Mr. Knight's steward; but by some additions to the house, and some judicious planting and skreening, it was made a pleasant and commodious abode. Mr. Knight was experienced and adroit at such arrangements, and this was a labour of love to him. A good-sized entrance and two sitting-rooms made the length of the house, all intended originally to look upon the road, but the large drawing-room window was blocked up and turned into a book-case, and another opened at the side which gave to view only turf and trees, as a high wooden fence and hornbeam hedge shut out the Winchester road, which skirted the whole length of the little domain. Trees were planted each side to form a shrubbery walk, carried round the enclosure, which gave a sufficient space for ladies' exercise. There was a pleasant irregular mixture of hedgerow, and gravel walk, and orchard, and long grass for mowing, arising from two or three little enclosures having been thrown together. The house itself was quite as good as the generality of parsonage-houses then were, and much in the same style; and was capable of receiving other members of the family as frequent visitors. It was sufficiently well furnished; everything inside and out was kept in good repair, and it was altogether a comfortable and ladylike establishment, though the means which supported it were not large.

I give this description because some interest is generally taken in the residence of a popular writer. Cowper's unattractive house in the street of Olney has been pointed out to visitors, and has even attained the honour of an engraving in Southey's edition of his works:[36] but I cannot recommend any admirer of Jane Austen to undertake a pilgrimage to this spot. The building indeed still stands, but it has lost all that gave it its character. After the death of Mrs. Cassandra Austen, in 1845, it was divided into tenements for labourers, and the grounds reverted to ordinary uses.

---

36 [Robert Southey, 1774–1843, was an English poet and the editor of *The works of William Cowper, Esq., comprising his poems, correspondence and translations. With a life of the author by the editor*, published in 1836 (and consisting of 15 volumes). Cowper, 1731–1800, was an English poet and hymn writer.]

CHAWTON HOUSE

Jane Austen's House Chawton M

CHAWTON COTTAGE

Chapter V

Description of Jane Austen's person, character, and tastes.

A S MY MEMOIR HAS now reached the period when I saw a great deal of my aunt, and was old enough to understand something of her value, I will here attempt a description of her person, mind, and habits. In person she was very attractive; her figure was rather tall and slender, her step light and firm, and her whole appearance expressive of health and animation. In complexion she was a clear brunette with a rich colour; she had full round cheeks, with mouth and nose small and well formed, bright hazel eyes, and brown hair forming natural curls close round her face. If not so regularly handsome as her sister, yet her countenance had a peculiar charm of its own to the eyes of most beholders. At the time of which I am now writing, she never was seen, either morning or evening, without a cap; I believe that she and her sister were generally thought to have taken to the garb of middle age earlier than their years or their looks required; and that, though remarkably neat in their dress as in all their ways, they were scarcely sufficiently regardful of the fashionable, or the becoming.

She was not highly accomplished according to the present standard. Her sister drew well, and it is from a drawing of hers that the likeness prefixed to this volume has been taken. Jane herself was fond of music, and had a sweet voice, both in singing and in conversation; in her youth she had received some instruction on the pianoforte; and at Chawton she practised daily, chiefly before breakfast. I believe she did so partly that she might not disturb the rest of the party who were less fond of music. In the evening she would sometimes sing, to her own accompaniment, some simple old songs, the words and airs of which, now never heard, still linger in my memory.

She read French with facility, and knew something of Italian. In those days German was no more thought of than Hindostanee,[37] as part of a lady's education. In history she followed the old guides—Goldsmith, Hume, and Robertson. Critical enquiry into the usually received statements of the old historians was scarcely begun. The history of the early kings of Rome had not yet been dissolved into legend. Historic charac-

---

37 [Hindustani: a dialect of Hindi widely spoken in India.]

ters lay before the reader's eyes in broad light or shade, not much broken up by details. The virtues of King Henry VIII were yet undiscovered, nor had much light been thrown on the inconsistencies of Queen Elizabeth; the one was held to be an unmitigated tyrant, and an embodied Blue Beard; the other a perfect model of wisdom and policy. Jane, when a girl, had strong political opinions, especially about the affairs of the sixteenth and seventeenth centuries. She was a vehement defender of Charles I and his grandmother Mary; but I think it was rather from an impulse of feeling than from any enquiry into the evidences by which they must be condemned or acquitted. As she grew up, the politics of the day occupied very little of her attention, but she probably shared the feeling of moderate Toryism which prevailed in her family. She was well acquainted with the old periodicals from the *Spectator* downwards. Her knowledge of Richardson's works was such as no one is likely again to acquire, now that the multitude and the merits of our light literature have called off the attention of readers from that great master. Every circumstance narrated in Sir Charles Grandison, all that was ever said or done in the cedar parlour, was familiar to her; and the wedding days of Lady L. and Lady G. were as well remembered as if they had been living friends. Amongst her favourite writers, Johnson in prose, Crabbe in verse, and Cowper in both, stood high. It is well that the native good taste of herself and of those with whom she lived, saved her from the snare into which a sister novelist had fallen, of imitating the grandiloquent style of Johnson. She thoroughly enjoyed Crabbe; perhaps on account of a certain resemblance to herself in minute and highly finished detail; and would sometimes say, in jest, that, if she ever married at all, she could fancy being Mrs. Crabbe; looking on the author quite as an abstract idea, and ignorant and regardless what manner of man he might be. Scott's poetry gave her great pleasure; she did not live to make much acquaintance with his novels. Only three of them were published before her death; but it will be seen by the following extract from one of her letters, that she was quite prepared to admit the merits of *Waverley*; and it is remarkable that, living, as she did, far apart from the gossip of the literary world, she should even then have spoken so confidently of his being the author of it:—

'Walter Scott has no business to write novels; especially good ones. It is not fair. He has fame and profit enough as a poet, and ought not to be taking the bread out of other people's mouths. I do not mean to like *Waverley*, if I can help it, but I fear I must. I am quite determined, however, not to be pleased with Mrs. —'s, should I ever meet with it, which I hope I may not. I think I can be stout against anything written by her. I have made up my mind to like no novels really, but Miss Edgeworth's, E.'s, and my own.'

It was not, however, what she *knew*, but what she *was*, that distinguished her from others. I cannot better describe the fascination which she exercised over children than by quoting the words of two of her nieces. One says:—

'As a very little girl I was always creeping up to aunt Jane, and following her whenever I could, in the house and out of it. I might not have remembered this but for the recollection of my mother's telling me privately, that I must not be troublesome to my aunt. Her first charm to children was great sweetness of manner. She seemed to love you, and you loved her in return. This, as well as I can now recollect, was what I felt in my early days, before I was old enough to be amused by her cleverness. But soon came the delight of her playful talk. She could make everything amusing to a child. Then, as I got older, when cousins came to share the entertainment, she would tell us the most delightful stories, chiefly of Fairyland, and her fairies had all characters of their own. The tale was invented, I am sure, at the moment, and was continued for two or three days, if occasion served.'

Again: 'When staying at Chawton, with two of her other nieces, we often had amusements in which my aunt was very helpful. She was the one to whom we always looked for help. She would furnish us with what we wanted from her wardrobe; and she would be the entertaining visitor in our make-believe house. She amused us in various ways. Once, I remember, in giving a conversation as between myself and my two cousins, supposing we were all grown up, the day after a ball.'

Very similar is the testimony of another niece:—'Aunt Jane was the general favourite with children; her ways with them being so playful, and her long circumstantial stories so delightful. These were continued from time to time, and were begged for on all possible and impossible occasions; woven, as she proceeded, out of nothing but her own happy talent for invention. Ah! if but one of them could be recovered! And again, as I grew older, when the original seventeen years between our ages seemed to shrink to seven, or to nothing, it comes back to me now how strangely I missed her. It had become so much a habit with me to put by things in my mind with a reference to her, and to say to myself, I shall keep this for aunt Jane.'

A nephew of hers used to observe that his visits to Chawton, after the death of his aunt Jane, were always a disappointment to him. From old associations he could not help expecting to be particularly happy in that house; and never till he got there could he realise to himself how all its peculiar charm was gone. It was not only that the chief light in the house was quenched, but that the loss of it had cast a shade over the spirits of the survivors. Enough has been said to show her love for children, and her wonderful power of entertaining them; but her friends of all ages felt her enlivening influence. Her unusually quick sense of the ridiculous led her to play with all the common-places of everyday life, whether as regarded persons or things; but she never played with its serious duties or responsibilities, nor did she ever turn individuals into ridicule. With all her neighbours in the village she vas on friendly, though not on intimate, terms. She took a kindly interest in all their proceedings, and liked to hear about them. They often served for her amusement; but it was her own nonsense that gave zest to the gossip. She was as far as possible from being censorious or satirical. She never abused them or *quizzed* them—*that* was the word of the day; an ugly word, now obsolete; and the ugly practice which it expressed is much less prevalent now than it was then. The laugh which she occasionally raised was by imagining for her neighbours, as she was equally ready to imagine for her friends or herself, impossible contingencies, or by relating in prose or verse some trifling anecdote coloured to her own fancy, or in writing a fictitious history of what they were supposed to have said or done, which could deceive nobody.

The following specimens may be given of the liveliness of mind which imparted an agreeable flavour both to her correspondence and her conversation:—

ON READING IN THE NEWSPAPERS THE MARRIAGE OF MR. GELL TO MISS GILL, OF EASTBOURNE.

At Eastbourne Mr. Gell, From being perfectly well,
Became dreadfully ill, For love of Miss Gill.
So he said, with some sighs, I'm the slave of your *iis*;
Oh, restore, if you please, By accepting my *ees*.

On the marriage of a middle-aged Flirt with a Mr. Wake, whom,
it was supposed, she would scarcely have accepted in her youth.

Maria, good-humoured, and handsome, and tall,
   For a husband was at her last stake;
And having in vain danced at many a ball,
   Is now happy to *jump at a Wake*.

'We were all at the play last night to see Miss O'Neil in Isabella. I do not think she was quite equal to my expectation. I fancy I want something more than can be. Acting seldom satisfies me. I took two pockethandkerchiefs, but had very little occasion for either. She is an elegant creature, however, and hugs Mr. Young delightfully.'

'So, Miss B. is actually married, but I have never seen it in the papers; and one may as well be single if the wedding is not to be in print.'

Once, too, she took it into her head to write the following mock panegyric on a young friend, who really was clever and handsome:—

1.

In measured verse I'll now rehearse
   The charms of lovely Anna:
And, first, her mind is unconfined
   Like any vast savannah.

2.

Ontario's lake may fitly speak
   Her fancy's ample bound:
Its circuit may, on strict survey
   Five hundred miles be found.

3.

Her wit descends on foes and friends
   Like famed Niagara's Fall;
And travellers gaze in wild amaze,
   And listen, one and all.

4.

Her judgment sound, thick, black, profound,
    Like transatlantic groves,
Dispenses aid, and friendly shade
    To all that in it roves.

5.

If thus her mind to be defined
    America exhausts,
And all that's grand in that great land
    In similes it costs—

6.

Oh how can I her person try
    To image and portray?
How paint the face, the form how trace
    In which those virtues lay?

7.

Another world must be unfurled,
    Another language known,
Ere tongue or sound can publish round
    Her charms of flesh and bone.

I believe that all this nonsense was nearly extempore, and that the fancy of drawing the images from America arose at the moment from the obvious rhyme which presented itself in the first stanza.

The following extracts are from letters addressed to a niece who was at that time amusing herself by attempting a novel, probably never finished, certainly never published, and of which I know nothing but what these extracts tell. They show the good-natured sympathy and encouragement which the aunt, then herself occupied in writing *Emma*, could give to the less matured powers of the niece. They bring out incidentally some of her opinions concerning compositions of that kind:—

Extracts.

'Chawton, Aug. 10, 1814.

'Your aunt C. does not like desultory novels, and is rather fearful that yours will be too much so; that there will be too frequent a change from one set of people to another, and that circumstances will be sometimes introduced, of apparent consequence, which will lead to nothing. It will not be so great an objection to me. I allow much more latitude than she does, and think nature and spirit cover many sins of a wandering story. And people in general do not care much about it, for your comfort ... '

'Sept. 9.

'You are now collecting your people delightfully, getting them exactly into such a spot as is the delight of my life. Three or four families in a country village is the very thing to work on; and I hope you will write a great deal more, and make full use of them while they are so very favourably arranged.'

'Sept. 28.

'Devereux Forrester being ruined by his vanity is very good: but I wish you would not let him plunge into a "vortex of dissipation." I do not object to the thing, but I cannot bear the expression: it is such thorough novel slang; and so old that I dare say Adam met with it in the first novel that he opened.'

'Hans Place (Nov. 1814).

'I have been very far from finding your book an evil, I assure you. I read it immediately, and with great pleasure. Indeed, I do think you get on very fast. I wish other people of my acquaintance could compose as rapidly. Julian's history was quite a surprise to me. You had not very long known it yourself, I suspect; but I have no objection to make to the circumstance; it is very well told, and his having been in love with the aunt gives Cecilia an additional interest with him. I like the idea; a very proper compliment to an aunt! I rather imagine, indeed, that nieces are seldom chosen but in compliment to some aunt or other. I dare say your husband was in love with me once, and would never have thought of you if he had not supposed me dead of a scarlet fever.'

Jane Austen was successful in everything that she attempted with her fingers. None of us could throw spilikins in so perfect a circle, or take them off with so steady a hand. Her performances with cup and ball were marvellous. The one used at Chawton was an easy one, and she has been known to catch it on the point above an hundred times in succession, till her hand was weary. She sometimes found a resource in that simple game, when unable, from weakness in her eyes, to read or write long together. A specimen of her clear strong handwriting is here given. Happy would the compositors for the press be if they had always so legible a manuscript to work from. But the writing was not the only part of her letters which showed superior handiwork. In those days there was an art in folding and sealing. No adhesive envelopes made all easy. Some people's letters always looked loose and untidy; but her paper was sure to take the right folds, and her sealing-wax to drop into the right place. Her needlework both plain and ornamental was excellent, and might almost have put a sewing machine to shame. She was considered especially great in satin stitch. She spent much time in these occupations, and some of her merriest talk was over clothes which she and her companions were making, sometimes for themselves, and sometimes for the poor. There still remains a curious specimen of her needlework made for a sister-in-law, my mother. In a very small bag is deposited a little rolled up housewife, furnished with minikin[38] needles and fine thread. In the housewife is a tiny pocket, and in the pocket is enclosed a slip of paper, on which, written as with a crow quill, are these lines:—

> This little bag, I hope, will prove
>   To be not vainly made;
> For should you thread and needles want,
>   It will afford you aid.

> And, as we are about to part,
>   'T will serve another end:
> For, when you look upon this bag,
>   You'll recollect your friend.

It is the kind of article that some benevolent fairy might be supposed to give as a reward to a diligent little girl. The whole is of flowered silk, and having been never used and carefully preserved, it is as fresh and bright as when it was first made seventy years ago; and shows that the same hand which painted so exquisitely with the pen could work as delicately with the needle.

I have collected some of the bright qualities which shone, as it were, on the surface of Jane Austen's character, and attracted most notice; but underneath them there lay the strong foundations of sound sense and judgment, rectitude of principle, and delicacy of feeling, qualifying her

---

38 [Small.]

equally to advise, assist, or amuse. She was, in fact, as ready to comfort the unhappy, or to nurse the sick, as she was to laugh and jest with the lighthearted. Two of her nieces were grown up, and one of them was married, before she was taken away from them. As their minds became more matured, they were admitted into closer intimacy with her, and learned more of her graver thoughts; they know what a sympathising friend and judicious adviser they found her to be in many little difficulties and doubts of early womanhood.

I do not venture to speak of her religious principles: that is a subject on which she herself was more inclined to *think* and *act* than to *talk*, and I shall imitate her reserve; satisfied to have shown how much of Christian love and humility abounded in her heart, without presuming to lay bare the roots whence those graces grew. Some little insight, however, into these deeper recesses of the heart must be given, when we come to speak of her death.

Chapter VI

Habits of Composition resumed after a long interval—First publication—The interest taken by the Author in the success of her Works.

IT MAY SEEM EXTRAORDINARY that Jane Austen should have written so little during the years that elapsed between leaving Steventon and settling at Chawton; especially when this cessation from work is contrasted with her literary activity both before and after that period. It might rather have been expected that fresh scenes and new acquaintance would have called forth her powers; while the quiet life which the family led both at Bath and Southampton must have afforded abundant leisure for composition; but so it was that nothing which I know of, certainly nothing which the public have seen, was completed in either of those places. I can only state the fact, without assigning any cause for it; but as soon as she was fixed in her second home, she resumed the habits of composition which had been formed in her first, and continued them to the end of her life. The first year of her residence at Chawton seems to have been devoted to revising and preparing for the press *Sense and Sensibility*, and *Pride and Prejudice*; but between February 1811 and August 1816, she began and completed *Mansfield Park*, *Emma*, and *Persuasion*, so that the last five years of her life produced the same number of novels with those which had been written in her early youth. How she was able to effect all this is surprising, for she had no separate study to retire to, and most of the work must have been done in the general sitting-room, subject to all kinds of casual interruptions. She was careful that her occupation should not be suspected by servants, or visitors, or any persons beyond her own family party. She wrote upon small sheets of paper which could easily be put away, or covered with a piece of blotting paper. There was, between the front door and the offices, a swing door which creaked when it was opened; but she objected to having this little inconvenience remedied, because it gave her notice when anyone was coming. She was not, however, troubled with companions like her own Mrs. Allen in *Northanger Abbey*, whose 'vacancy of mind and incapacity for thinking were such that, as she never talked a great deal, so she could never be entirely silent; and therefore, while she sat at work, if she lost her needle, or broke her thread, or saw a speck of dirt on her gown, she must observe it, whether there were any one at leisure to answer her or not.' In that well occupied female party there must have been many precious hours of silence during which the pen was busy at the little mahogany writing-desk,[39] while Fanny Price, or Emma Woodhouse, or Anne Elliott was growing into beauty and interest. I have no doubt that I, and my sisters and cousins, in our visits to Chawton, frequently disturbed this mystic process, without having any idea of the mischief that we were doing; certainly we never should have guessed it by any signs of impatience or irritability in the writer.

As so much had been previously prepared, when once she began to publish, her works came out in quick succession. *Sense and Sensibility* was published in 1811, *Pride and Prejudice* at the beginning of 1813, *Mansfield Park* in 1814, *Emma* early in 1816; *Northanger Abbey* and *Persuasion* did not appear till after her death, in 1818. It will be shown farther on why *Northanger Abbey*, though amongst the first written, was one of the last published. Her first three novels were published by Egerton, her last three by Murray.[40] The profits of the four which had been printed before her death had not at that time amounted to seven hundred pounds.

I have no record of the publication of *Sense and Sensibility*, nor of the author's feelings at this her first appearance before the public; but the following extracts from three letters to her sister give a lively picture of the interest with which she watched the reception of *Pride and Prejudice*, and show the carefulness with which she corrected her compositions, and rejected much that had been written:—

Chawton, Friday, January 29 (1813).

'I hope you received my little parcel by J. Bond on Wednesday evening, my dear Cassandra, and that you will be ready to hear from me again on Sunday, for I feel that I must write to you to-day. I want to tell you that I have got my own darling child from London. On Wednesday I received one copy sent down by Falkener, with three lines from Henry to say that he had given another to Charles and sent a third by the coach to Godmersham ... The advertisement is in our paper to-day for

---

39 This mahogany desk, which has done good service to the public, is now in the possession of my sister, Miss Austen.
40 [John Murray, a well-known publisher of the time.]

the first time: 18s.[41] He shall ask £1. 1s. for my two next, and £1. 8s. for my stupidest of all. Miss B. dined with us on the very day of the book's coming, and in the evening we fairly set at it, and read half the first vol. to her, prefacing that, having intelligence from Henry that such a work would soon appear, we had desired him to send it whenever it came out, and I believe it passed with her unsuspected. She was amused, poor soul! *That* she could not help, you know, with two such people to lead the way, but she really does seem to admire Elizabeth. I must confess that I think her as delightful a creature as ever appeared in print, and how I shall be able to tolerate those who do not like *her* at least I do not know. There are a few typical errors; and a "said he," or a "said she," would sometimes make the dialogue more immediately clear; but "I do not write for such dull elves" as have not a great deal of ingenuity themselves. The second volume is shorter than I could wish, but the difference is not so much in reality as in look, there being a larger proportion of narrative in that part. I have lop't and crop't so successfully, however, that I imagine it must be rather shorter than *Sense and Sensibility* altogether. Now I will try and write of something else.'

Chawton, Thursday, February 4 (1813).

'My dear Cassandra,—Your letter was truly welcome, and I am much obliged to you for all your praise; it came at a right time, for I had had some fits of disgust. Our second evening's reading to Miss B. had not pleased me so well, but I believe something must be attributed to my mother's too rapid way of getting on: though she perfectly understands the characters herself, she cannot speak as they ought. Upon the whole, however, I am quite vain enough and well satisfied enough. The work is rather too light, and bright, and sparkling; it wants shade; it wants to be stretched out here and there with a long chapter of sense, if it could be had; if not, of solemn specious nonsense, about something unconnected with the story; an essay on writing, a critique on Walter Scott, or the history of Buonaparté, or something that would form a contrast, and bring the reader with increased delight to the playfulness and epigrammatism of the general style ... The greatest blunder in the printing that I have met with is in page 220, v. 3, where two speeches

---

41 [Eighteen shillings: there were 20 shillings to the pound.]

are made into one. There might as well be no suppers at Longbourn; but I suppose it was the remains of Mrs. Bennett's old Meryton habits.'

The following letter seems to have been written soon after the last two: in February 1813:—

'This will be a quick return for yours, my dear Cassandra; I doubt its having much else to recommend it; but there is no saying; it may turn out to be a very long and delightful letter. I am exceedingly pleased that you can say what you do, after having gone through the whole work, and Fanny's praise is very gratifying. My hopes were tolerably strong of *her*, but nothing like a certainty. Her liking Darcy and Elizabeth is enough. She might hate all the others, if she would. I have her opinion under her own hand this morning, but your transcript of it, which I read first, was not, and is not, the less acceptable. To *me* it is of course all praise, but the more exact truth which she sends you is good enough ... Our party on Wednesday was not unagreeable, though we wanted a master of the house less anxious and fidgety, and more conversable. Upon Mrs. —'s mentioning that she had sent the rejected addresses to Mrs. H., I began talking to her a little about them, and expressed my hope of their having amused her. Her answer was, "Oh dear yes, very much, very droll indeed, the opening of the house, and the striking up of the fiddles!" What she meant, poor woman, who shall say? I sought no farther. As soon as a whist party was formed, and a round table threatened, I made my mother an excuse and came away, leaving just as many for *their* round table as there were at Mrs. Grant's.[42] I wish they might be as agreeable a set. My mother is very well, and finds great amusement in glove-knitting, and at present wants no other work. We quite run over with books. She has got Sir John Carr's *Travels in Spain*, and I am reading a Society octavo, an *Essay on the Military Police and Institutions of the British Empire*, by Capt. Pasley of the Engineers, a book which I protested against at first, but which upon trial I find delightfully written and highly entertaining. I am as much in love with the author as I ever was with Clarkson or Buchanan, or even the two Mr. Smiths of the city. The first soldier I ever sighed for; but he does write with extraordinary force and spirit. Yesterday, moreover,

---

42 At this time, February 1813, *Mansfield Park* was nearly finished.

brought us *Mrs. Grant's Letters*, with Mr. White's compliments; but I have disposed of them, compliments and all, to Miss P., and amongst so many readers or retainers of books as we have in Chawton, I dare say there will be no difficulty in getting rid of them for another fortnight, if necessary. I have disposed of Mrs. Grant for the second fortnight to Mrs. —. It can make no difference to *her* which of the twenty-six fortnights in the year the 3 vols. lie on her table. I have been applied to for information as to the oath taken in former times of Bell, Book, and Candle, but have none to give. Perhaps you may be able to learn something of its origin where you now are. Ladies who read those enormous great stupid thick quarto[43] volumes which one always sees in the breakfast parlour there must be acquainted with everything in the world. I detest a quarto. Capt. Pasley's book is too good for their society. They will not understand a man who condenses his thoughts into an octavo.[44] I have learned from Sir J. Carr that there is no Government House at Gibraltar. I must alter it to the Commissioner's.'

The following letter belongs to the same year, but treats of a different subject. It describes a journey from Chawton to London, in her brother's curricle, and shows how much could be seen and enjoyed in course of a long summer's day by leisurely travelling amongst scenery which the traveller in an express train now rushes through in little more than an hour, but scarcely sees at all:—

'Sloane Street, Thursday, May 20 (1813).

'My dear Cassandra,

'Before I say anything else, I claim a paper full of halfpence on the drawing-room mantel-piece; I put them there myself, and forgot to bring them with me. I cannot say that I have yet been in any distress for money, but I chuse to have my due, as well as the Devil. How lucky we were in our weather yesterday! This wet morning makes one more sensible of it. We had no rain of any consequence. The head of the curricle was put half up three or four times, but our share of the showers was very trifling, though they seemed to be heavy all round us, when we were on the Hog's-back, and I fancied it might then be raining so hard at Chawton as to make you

---

43 [Quarto, referring to a book's size could be as large as 12 inches tall.]
44 [Probably slightly smaller than the size of the present book.]

feel for us much more than we deserved. Three hours and a quarter took us to Guildford, where we staid barely two hours, and had only just time enough for all we had to do there; that is, eating a long and comfortable breakfast, watching the carriages, paying Mr. Harrington, and taking a little stroll afterwards. From some views which that stroll gave us, I think most highly of the situation of Guildford. We wanted all our brothers and sisters to be standing with us in the bowling-green, and looking towards Horsham. I was very lucky in my gloves—got them at the first shop I went to, though I went into it rather because it was near than because it looked at all like a glove shop, and gave only four shillings for them; after which everybody at Chawton will be hoping and predicting that they cannot be good for anything, and their worth certainly remains to be proved; but I think they look very well. We left Guildford at twenty minutes before twelve (I hope somebody cares for these minutiæ), and were at Esher in about two hours more. I was very much pleased with the country in general. Between Guildford and Ripley I thought it particularly pretty, also about Painshill; and from a Mr. Spicer's grounds at Esher, which we walked into before dinner, the views were beautiful. I cannot say what we did not see, but I should think there could not be a wood, or a meadow, or palace, or remarkable spot in England that was not spread out before us on one side or other. Claremont is going to be sold: a Mr. Ellis has it now. It is a house that seems never to have prospered. After dinner we walked forward to be overtaken at the coachman's time, and before he did overtake us we were very near Kingston. I fancy it was about half-past six when we reached this house—a twelve hours' business, and the horses did not appear more than reasonably tired. I was very tired too, and glad to get to bed early, but am quite well to-day. I am very snug in the front drawing-room all to myself, and would not say "thank you" for any company but you. The quietness of it does me good. I have contrived to pay my two visits, though the weather made me a great while about it, and left me only a few minutes to sit with Charlotte Craven.[45] She looks very well, and her hair is done up with an elegance to do credit to any education. Her manners are as unaffected and pleasing as ever. She had heard from her mother to-day. Mrs. Craven spends another fortnight at Chilton. I saw nobody but Charlotte, which pleased me best. I was shewn upstairs into a drawing-room, where she came to me, and the appear-

---

45 The present Lady Pollen, of Redenham, near Andover, then at a school in London.

ance of the room, so totally unschool-like, amused me very much; it was full of modern elegancies.

'Yours very affec^{tly}.,

'J.A.'

The next letter, written in the following year, contains an account of another journey to London, with her brother Henry, and reading with him the manuscript of *Mansfield Park*:—

'Henrietta Street, Wednesday, March 2 (1814).

'My dear Cassandra,

'You were wrong in thinking of us at Guildford last night: we were at Cobham. On reaching G. we found that John and the horses were gone on. We therefore did no more than we had done at Farnham—sit in the carriage while fresh horses were put in, and proceeded directly to Cobham, which we reached by seven, and about eight were sitting down to a very nice roast fowl, &c. We had altogether a very good journey, and everything at Cobham was comfortable. I could not pay Mr. Harrington! That was the only alas! of the business. I shall therefore return his bill, and my mother's £2, that you may try your luck. We did not begin reading till Bentley Green. Henry's approbation is hitherto even equal to my wishes. He says it is different from the other two, but does not appear to think it at all inferior. He has only married Mrs. R. I am afraid he has gone through the most entertaining part. He took to Lady B. and Mrs. N. most kindly, and gives great praise to the drawing of the characters. He understands them all, likes Fanny, and, I think, foresees how it will all be. I finished the *Heroine*[46] last night, and was very much amused by it. I wonder James did not like it better. It diverted me exceedingly. We went to bed at ten. I was very tired, but slept to a miracle, and am lovely to-day, and at present Henry seems to have no complaint. We left Cobham at half-past eight, stopped to bait and breakfast at Kingston, and were in this house considerably before two. Nice smiling Mr. Barlowe met us at the door and, in reply to enquiries after news, said that peace was generally expected. I have taken possession of my bedroom, unpacked my bandbox, sent Miss P.'s two letters to the twopenny post, been visited by M^d. B., and am now writing by

---

46 [*The Heroine: or, Adventures of Cherubina* by Eaton Stannard Barrett, 1786–1820, published in 1813. The book is a satire of Gothic novels.]

myself at the new table in the front room. It is snowing. We had some snowstorms yesterday, and a smart frost at night, which gave us a hard road from Cobham to Kingston; but as it was then getting dirty and heavy, Henry had a pair of leaders put on to the bottom of Sloane St. His own horses, therefore, cannot have had hard work. I watched for *veils* as we drove through the streets, and had the pleasure of seeing several upon vulgar heads. And now, how do you all do?—you in particular, after the worry of yesterday and the day before. I hope Martha had a pleasant visit again, and that you and my mother could eat your beef-pudding. Depend upon my thinking of the chimney-sweeper as soon as I wake to-morrow. Places are secured at Drury Lane for Saturday, but so great is the rage for seeing Kean that only a third and fourth row could be got; as it is in a front box, however, I hope we shall do pretty well—Shylock, a good play for Fanny—she cannot be much affected, I think. Mrs. Perigord has just been here. She tells me that we owe her master for the silk-dyeing. My poor old muslin has never been dyed yet. It has been promised to be done several times. What wicked people dyers are. They begin with dipping their own souls in scarlet sin. It is evening. We have drank tea, and I have torn through the third vol. of the *Heroine*. I do not think it falls off. It is a delightful burlesque, particularly on the Radcliffe[47] style. Henry is going on with *Mansfield Park*. He admires H. Crawford: I mean properly, as a clever, pleasant man. I tell you all the good I can, as I know how much you will enjoy it. We hear that Mr. Kean is more admired than ever. There are no good places to be got in Drury Lane for the next fortnight, but Henry means to secure some for Saturday fortnight, when you are reckoned upon. Give my love to little Cass. I hope she found my bed comfortable last night. I have seen nobody in London yet with such a long chin as Dr. Syntax,[48] nor anybody quite so large as Gogmagolicus.[49]

'Yours aff^ly.

'J. Austen.'

---

47 [Ann Radcliffe, 1764–1823, an English author noted for her Gothic novels.]
48 [*The Tour of Doctor Syntax in search of the picturesque* by William Combe, published in book form in 1812. The book featured drawings and Dr. Syntax is featured with a long chin.]
49 [A legendary giant.]

Chapter VII

Seclusion from the literary world—Notice from the Prince Regent—Correspondence with Mr. Clarke—Suggestions to alter her style of writing.

JANE AUSTEN LIVED IN entire seclusion from the literary world: neither by correspondence, nor by personal intercourse was she known to any contemporary authors. It is probable that she never was in company with any person whose talents or whose celebrity equalled her own; so that her powers never could have been sharpened by collision with superior intellects, nor her imagination aided by their casual suggestions. Whatever she produced was a genuine home-made article. Even during the last two or three years of her life, when her works were rising in the estimation of the public, they did not enlarge the circle of her acquaintance. Few of her readers knew even her name, and none knew more of her than her name. I doubt whether it would be possible to mention any other author of note, whose personal obscurity was so complete. I can think of none like her, but of many to contrast with her in that respect. Fanny Burney, afterwards Madame D'Arblay, was at an early age petted by Dr. Johnson, and introduced to the wits and scholars of the day at the tables of Mrs. Thrale and Sir Joshua Reynolds. Anna Seward, in her self-constituted shrine at Lichfield, would have been miserable, had she not trusted that the eyes of all lovers of poetry were devoutly fixed on her. Joanna Baillie and Maria Edgeworth were indeed far from courting publicity; they loved the privacy of their own families, one with her brother and sister in their Hampstead villa, the other in her more distant retreat in Ireland; but fame pursued them, and they were the favourite correspondents of Sir Walter Scott. Crabbe, who was usually buried in a country parish, yet sometimes visited London, and dined at Holland House, and was received as a fellow-poet by Campbell, Moore, and Rogers; and on one memorable occasion he was Scott's guest at Edinburgh, and gazed with wondering eyes on the incongruous pageantry with which George IV was entertained in that city. Even those great writers who hid themselves amongst lakes and mountains associated with each other; and though little seen by the world were so much in its thoughts that a new term, 'Lakers,' was coined to designate them. The chief part of Charlotte Brontë's life was spent in a wild solitude compared with which Steventon and Chawton might be considered to be in the gay world; and yet she attained to personal distinction which never fell to Jane's lot. When she visited her kind publisher in London, literary men and women were invited purposely to meet her: Thackeray bestowed upon her the honour of his notice; and once in Willis's Rooms,[50] she had to walk shy and trembling through an avenue of lords and ladies, drawn up for the purpose of gazing at the author of *Jane Eyre*. Miss Mitford, too, lived quietly in *Our Village*,[51] devoting her time and talents to the benefit of a father scarcely worthy of her; but she did not live there unknown. Her tragedies gave her a name in London. She numbered Milman and Talfourd amongst her correspondents; and her works were a passport to the society of many who would not otherwise have sought her. Hundreds admired Miss Mitford on account of her writings for one who ever connected the idea of Miss Austen with the press. A few years ago, a gentleman visiting Winchester Cathedral desired to be shown Miss Austen's grave. The verger, as he pointed it out, asked, 'Pray, sir, can you tell me whether there was anything particular about that lady; so many people want to know where she was buried?' During her life the ignorance of the verger was shared by most people; few knew that 'there was anything particular about that lady.'

It was not till towards the close of her life, when the last of the works that she saw published was in the press, that she received the only mark of distinction ever bestowed upon her; and that was remarkable for the high quarter whence it emanated rather than for any actual increase of fame that it conferred. It happened thus. In the autumn of 1815 she nursed her brother Henry through a dangerous fever and slow convalescence at his house in Hans Place. He was attended by one of the Prince Regent's physicians. All attempts to keep her name secret had at this time ceased, and though it had never appeared on a title-page, all who cared to know might easily learn it: and the friendly physician was aware that his patient's nurse was the author of *Pride and Prejudice*.

---

50 See Mrs. Gaskell's *Life of Miss Brontë*, vol. ii. p. 215. [Elizabeth Gaskell, 1810–65, English novelist, *The Life of Charlotte Brontë*, 1857.]
51 [Mary Russell Mitford, 1787–1855, was an English writer. *Our Village: Sketches of Rural Character and Scenery* was a series of short stories published from the 1820s to the 1830s.]

Accordingly he informed her one day that the Prince was a great admirer of her novels; that he read them often, and kept a set in every one of
his residences; that he himself therefore had thought it right to inform
his Royal Highness that Miss Austen was staying in London, and that
the Prince had desired Mr. Clarke, the librarian of Carlton House, to
wait upon her. The next day Mr. Clarke made his appearance, and invited her to Carlton House, saying that he had the Prince's instructions to
show her the library and other apartments, and to pay her every possible
attention. The invitation was of course accepted, and during the visit to
Carlton House Mr. Clarke declared himself commissioned to say that if
Miss Austen had any other novel forthcoming she was at liberty to dedicate it to the Prince. Accordingly such a dedication was immediately
prefixed to *Emma*, which was at that time in the press.

Mr. Clarke was the brother of Dr. Clarke, the traveller and mineralo-
gist, whose life has been written by Bishop Otter. Jane found in him not
only a very courteous gentleman, but also a warm admirer of her talents; though it will be seen by his letters that he did not clearly appre-
hend the limits of her powers, or the proper field for their exercise. The
following correspondence took place between them.

Feeling some apprehension lest she should make a mistake in acting
on the verbal permission which she had received from the Prince, Jane
addressed the following letter to Mr. Clarke:—

'Nov. 15, 1815.

'Sir,—I must take the liberty of asking you a question. Among the
many flattering attentions which I received from you at Carlton House
on Monday last was the information of my being at liberty to dedicate
any future work to His Royal Highness the Prince Regent, without the
necessity of any solicitation on my part. Such, at least, I believed to be
your words; but as I am very anxious to be quite certain of what was
intended, I entreat you to have the goodness to inform me how such a
permission is to be understood, and whether it is incumbent on me to
show my sense of the honour, by inscribing the work now in the press
to His Royal Highness; I should be equally concerned to appear either
presumptuous or ungrateful.'

The following gracious answer was returned by Mr. Clarke, together
with a suggestion which must have been received with some surprise:—

'Carlton House, Nov. 16, 1815.

'Dear Madam,—It is certainly not *incumbent* on you to dedicate your work now in the press to His Royal Highness; but if you wish to do the Regent that honour either now or at any future period I am happy to send you that permission, which need not require any more trouble or solicitation on your part.

'Your late works, Madam, and in particular *Mansfield Park*, reflect the highest honour on your genius and your principles. In every new work your mind seems to increase its energy and power of discrimination. The Regent has read and admired all your publications.

'Accept my best thanks for the pleasure your volumes have given me. In the perusal of them I felt a great inclination to write and say so. And I also, dear Madam, wished to be allowed to ask you to delineate in some future work the habits of life, and character, and enthusiasm of a clergyman, who should pass his time between the metropolis and the country, who should be something like Beattie's Minstrel[52]—

> Silent when glad, affectionate tho' shy,
>   And in his looks was most demurely sad;
>   And now he laughed aloud, yet none knew why.

Neither Goldsmith, nor La Fontaine in his *Tableau de Famille*, have in my mind quite delineated an English clergyman, at least of the present day, fond of and entirely engaged in literature, no man's enemy but his own. Pray, dear Madam, think of these things.

'Believe me at all times with sincerity
and respect, your faithful and obliged servant,
'J. S. Clarke, Librarian.'

The following letter, written in reply, will show how unequal the author of *Pride and Prejudice* felt herself to delineating an enthusiastic clergyman of the present day, who should resemble Beattie's Minstrel:—

'Dec. 11.

'Dear Sir,—My *Emma* is now so near publication that I feel it right to assure you of my not having forgotten your kind recommendation of

---

52 [From *The Minstrel; or, The Progress of Genius* by James Beattie, 1735–1803, a Scottish poet.]

an early copy for Carlton House, and that I have Mr. Murray's promise of its being sent to His Royal Highness, under cover to you, three days previous to the work being really out. I must make use of this opportunity to thank you, dear Sir, for the very high praise you bestow on my other novels. I am too vain to wish to convince you that you have praised them beyond their merits. My greatest anxiety at present is that this fourth work should not disgrace what was good in the others. But on this point I will do myself the justice to declare that, whatever may be my wishes for its success, I am strongly haunted with the idea that to those readers who have preferred *Pride and Prejudice* it will appear inferior in wit, and to those who have preferred *Mansfield Park* inferior in good sense. Such as it is, however, I hope you will do me the favour of accepting a copy. Mr. Murray will have directions for sending one. I am quite honoured by your thinking me capable of drawing such a clergyman as you gave the sketch of in your note of Nov. 16th. But I assure you I am *not*. The comic part of the character I might be equal to, but not the good, the enthusiastic, the literary. Such a man's conversation must at times be on subjects of science and philosophy, of which I know nothing; or at least be occasionally abundant in quotations and allusions which a woman who, like me, knows only her own mother tongue, and has read little in that, would be totally without the power of giving. A classical education, or at any rate a very extensive acquaintance with English literature, ancient and modern, appears to me quite indispensable for the person who would do any justice to your clergyman; and I think I may boast myself to be, with all possible vanity, the most unlearned and uninformed female who ever dared to be an authoress.

'Believe me, dear Sir,

'Your obliged and faithful hum^bl Ser^t.

'Jane Austen.'[53]

Mr. Clarke, however, was not to be discouraged from proposing another subject. He had recently been appointed chaplain and private English secretary to Prince Leopold, who was then about to be united to the Princess Charlotte; and when he again wrote to express the

---

53 It was her pleasure to boast of greater ignorance than she had any just claim to. She knew more than her mother tongue, for she knew a good deal of French and a little of Italian.

gracious thanks of the Prince Regent for the copy of *Emma* which had been presented, he suggests that 'an historical romance illustrative of the august House of Cobourg would just now be very interesting,' and might very properly be dedicated to Prince Leopold. This was much as if Sir William Ross had been set to paint a great battle-piece; and it is amusing to see with what grave civility she declined a proposal which must have struck her as ludicrous, in the following letter:—

'My dear Sir,—I am honoured by the Prince's thanks and very much obliged to yourself for the kind manner in which you mention the work. I have also to acknowledge a former letter forwarded to me from Hans Place. I assure you I felt very grateful for the friendly tenor of it, and hope my silence will have been considered, as it was truly meant, to proceed only from an unwillingness to tax your time with idle thanks. Under every interesting circumstance which your own talents and literary labours have placed you in, or the favour of the Regent bestowed, you have my best wishes. Your recent appointments I hope are a step to something still better. In my opinion, the service of a court can hardly be too well paid, for immense must be the sacrifice of time and feeling required by it.

'You are very kind in your hints as to the sort of composition which might recommend me at present, and I am fully sensible that an historical romance, founded on the House of Saxe Cobourg, might be much more to the purpose of profit or popularity than such pictures of domestic life in country villages as I deal in. But I could no more write a romance than an epic poem. I could not sit seriously down to write a serious romance under any other motive than to save my life; and if it were indispensable for me to keep it up and never relax into laughing at myself or at other people, I am sure I should be hung before I had finished the first chapter. No, I must keep to my own style and go on in my own way; and though I may never succeed again in that, I am convinced that I should totally fail in any other.

'I remain, my dear Sir,
'Your very much obliged, and sincere friend,
'J. Austen.

'Chawton, near Alton, April 1, 1816.'

Mr. Clarke should have recollected the warning of the wise man, 'Force not the course of the river.' If you divert it from the channel in which nature taught it to flow, and force it into one arbitrarily cut by yourself, you will lose its grace and beauty.

> But when his free course is not hindered,
> He makes sweet music with the enamelled stones,
> Giving a gentle kiss to every sedge
> He overtaketh in his pilgrimage:
> And so by many winding nooks he strays
> With willing sport.[54]

All writers of fiction, who have genius strong enough to work out a course of their own, resist every attempt to interfere with its direction. No two writers could be more unlike each other than Jane Austen and Charlotte Brontë; so much so that the latter was unable to understand why the former was admired, and confessed that she herself 'should hardly like to live with her ladies and gentlemen, in their elegant but confined houses;' but each writer equally resisted interference with her own natural style of composition. Miss Brontë, in reply to a friendly critic, who had warned her against being too melodramatic, and had ventured to propose Miss Austen's works to her as a study, writes thus:—

'Whenever I *do* write another book, I think I will have nothing of what you call "melodrama." I *think* so, but I am not sure. I *think*, too, I will endeavour to follow the counsel which shines out of Miss Austen's "mild eyes," to finish more, and be more subdued; but neither am I sure of that. When authors write best, or, at least, when they write most fluently, an influence seems to waken in them which becomes their master—which will have its way—putting out of view all behests but its own, dictating certain words, and insisting on their being used, whether vehement or measured in their nature, new moulding characters, giving unthought of turns to incidents, rejecting carefully elaborated old ideas, and suddenly creating and adopting new ones. Is it not so? And should we try to counteract this influence? Can we indeed counteract it?'[55]

---

54 [From Shakespeare's *Two Gentleman of Verona*. (The first line is misquoted: 'But when his fair course is not hindered,').]
55 Mrs. Gaskell's *Life of Miss Brontë*, vol. ii. p. 53.

The playful raillery with which the one parries an attack on her liberty, and the vehement eloquence of the other in pleading the same cause and maintaining the independence of genius, are very characteristic of the minds of the respective writers.

The suggestions which Jane received as to the sort of story that she ought to write were, however, an amusement to her, though they were not likely to prove useful; and she has left amongst her papers one entitled, 'Plan of a novel according to hints from various quarters.' The names of some of those advisers are written on the margin of the manuscript opposite to their respective suggestions.

'Heroine to be the daughter of a clergyman, who after having lived much in the world had retired from it, and settled on a curacy with a very small fortune of his own. The most excellent man that can be imagined, perfect in character, temper, and manner, without the smallest drawback or peculiarity to prevent his being the most delightful companion to his daughter from one year's end to the other. Heroine faultless in character, beautiful in person, and possessing every possible accomplishment. Book to open with father and daughter conversing in long speeches, elegant language, and a tone of high serious sentiment. The father induced, at his daughter's earnest request, to relate to her the past events of his life. Narrative to reach through the greater part of the first volume; as besides all the circumstances of his attachment to her mother, and their marriage, it will comprehend his going to sea as chaplain to a distinguished naval character about the court; and his going afterwards to court himself, which involved him in many interesting situations, concluding with his opinion of the benefits of tithes being done away with ... From this outset the story will proceed, and contain a striking variety of adventures. Father an exemplary parish priest, and devoted to literature; but heroine and father never above a fortnight in one place: he being driven from his curacy by the vile arts of some totally unprincipled and heartless young man, desperately in love with the heroine, and pursuing her with unrelenting passion. No sooner settled in one country of Europe, than they are compelled to quit it, and retire to another, always making new acquaintance, and always obliged to leave them. This will of course exhibit a wide variety of character. The scene will be for ever shifting from one set of people to another, but there will be no mixture, all the good will be unexceptionable in every respect. There will be no foibles or weaknesses but with the wicked, who will be completely depraved and infamous, hardly a resemblance of humanity left in them. Early in her career, the heroine must meet with the hero: all perfection, of course, and only prevented from paying his addresses to her by some excess of refinement. Wherever she goes, somebody falls in love with her, and she receives repeated offers of marriage, which she refers wholly to her father, exceedingly angry that he should not be the first applied to. Often carried away by the anti-hero, but rescued either by her father or the hero. Often reduced to support herself and her father by her talents, and work for her bread; continually cheated, and defrauded of her hire; worn down to a skeleton, and now and then starved to death. At last, hunted out of civilised society, denied the poor shelter of the humblest cottage, they are compelled to retreat into Kamtschatka, where the poor father quite worn down, finding his end approaching, throws himself on the ground, and after four or five hours of tender advice and parental admonition to his miserable child, expires in a fine burst of literary enthusiasm, intermingled with invectives against the holders of tithes. Heroine inconsolable for some time, but afterwards crawls back towards her former country, having at least twenty narrow escapes of falling into the hands of anti-hero; and at last, in the very nick of time, turning a corner to avoid him, runs into the arms of the hero himself, who, having just shaken off the scruples which fettered him before, was at the very moment setting off in pursuit of her. The tenderest and completest *éclaircissement* takes place, and they are happily united. Throughout the whole work heroine to be in the most elegant society, and living in high style.'

Since the first publication of this memoir, Mr. Murray of Albemarle Street has very kindly sent to me copies of the following letters, which his father received from Jane Austen, when engaged in the publication of *Emma*. The increasing cordiality of the letters shows that the author felt that her interests were duly cared for, and was glad to find herself in the hands of a publisher whom she could consider as a friend.

Her brother had addressed to Mr. Murray a strong complaint of the tardiness of a printer:—

'23 Hans Place, Thursday, November 23 (1815).
'Sir,—My brother's note last Monday has been so fruitless, that I am afraid there can be but little chance of my writing to any good effect;

but yet I am so very much disappointed and vexed by the delays of the printers, that I cannot help begging to know whether there is no hope of their being quickened. Instead of the work being ready by the end of the present month, it will hardly, at the rate we now proceed, be finished by the end of the next; and as I expect to leave London early in December, it is of consequence that no more time should be lost. Is it likely that the printers will be influenced to greater dispatch and punctuality by knowing that the work is to be dedicated, by permission, to the Prince Regent? If you can make that circumstance operate, I shall be very glad. My brother returns *Waterloo* with many thanks for the loan of it. We have heard much of Scott's account of Paris.[56] If it be not incompatible with other arrangements, would you favour us with it, supposing you have any set already opened? You may depend upon its being in careful hands.

'I remain, Sir, your ob^t. humble Se^t.

'J. Austen.'

'Hans Place, December 11 (1815).

'Dear Sir,—As I find that *Emma* is advertised for publication as early as Saturday next, I think it best to lose no time in settling all that remains to be settled on the subject, and adopt this method as involving the smallest tax on your time.

'In the first place, I beg you to understand that I leave the terms on which the trade should be supplied with the work entirely to your judgment, entreating you to be guided in every such arrangement by your own experience of what is most likely to clear off the edition rapidly. I shall be satisfied with whatever you feel to be best. The title-page must be "Emma, dedicated by permission to H.R.H. the Prince Regent." And it is my particular wish that one set should be completed and sent to H.R.H. two or three days before the work is generally public. It should be sent under cover to the Rev. J. S. Clarke, Librarian, Carlton House. I shall subjoin a list of those persons to whom I must trouble you to forward also a set each, when the work is out; all unbound, with "From the Authoress" in the first page.

---

56 This must have been *Paul's Letters to his Kinsfolk*. [By Sir Walter Scott, published in 1816.]

'I return you, with very many thanks, the books you have so oblig-ingly supplied me with. I am very sensible, I assure you, of the atten-tion you have paid to my convenience and amusement. I return also *Mansfield Park,* as ready for a second edition, I believe, as I can make it. I am in Hans Place till the 16th. From that day inclusive, my direction will be Chawton, Alton, Hants.

'I remain, dear Sir,

'Y^r faithful humb. Servt.

'J. Austen.

'I wish you would have the goodness to send a line by the bearer, stating *the day* on which the set will be ready for the Prince Regent.'

'Hans Place, December 11 (1815).

'Dear Sir,—I am much obliged by yours, and very happy to feel eve-rything arranged to our mutual satisfaction. As to my direction about the title-page, it was arising from my ignorance only, and from my hav-ing never noticed the proper place for a dedication. I thank you for put-ting me right. Any deviation from what is usually done in such cases is the last thing I should wish for. I feel happy in having a friend to save me from the ill effect of my own blunder.

'Yours, dear Sir, &c.

'J. Austen.'

'Chawton, April 1, 1816.

'Dear Sir,—I return you the *Quarterly Review* with many thanks. The Authoress of *Emma* has no reason, I think, to complain of her treatment in it, except in the total omission of *Mansfield Park*. I cannot but be sorry that so clever a man as the Reviewer of *Emma* should con-sider it as unworthy of being noticed. You will be pleased to hear that I have received the Prince's thanks for the *handsome* copy I sent him of *Emma*. Whatever he may think of *my* share of the work, yours seems to have been quite right.

'In consequence of the late event in Henrietta Street, I must request that if you should at any time have anything to communicate by letter, you will be so good as to write by the post, directing to me (Miss J. Austen), Chawton, near Alton; and that for anything of a larg-er bulk, you will add to the same direction, by *Collier's Southampton coach.*

'I remain, dear Sir,
'Yours very faithfully,
'J. Austen.'

About the same time the following letters passed between the Countess of Morley and the writer of *Emma*. I do not know whether they were personally acquainted with each other, nor in what this interchange of civilities originated:—

The Countess of Morley to Miss J. Austen.

'Saltram, December 27 (1815).

'Madam,—I have been most anxiously waiting for an introduction to *Emma*, and am infinitely obliged to you for your kind recollection of me, which will procure me the pleasure of her acquaintance some days sooner than I should otherwise have had it. I am already become intimate with the Woodhouse family, and feel that they will not amuse and interest me less than the Bennetts, Bertrams, Norrises, and all their admirable predecessors. I can give them no higher praise.

'I am, Madam, your much obliged
'F. Morley.'

Miss J. Austen to the Countess of Morley.

'Madam,—Accept my thanks for the honour of your note, and for your kind disposition in favour of *Emma*. In my present state of doubt as to her reception in the world, it is particularly gratifying to me to receive so early an assurance of your Ladyship's approbation. It encourages me to depend on the same share of general good opinion which *Emma*'s predecessors have experienced, and to believe that I have not yet, as almost every writer of fancy does sooner or later, overwritten myself.

'I am, Madam,
'Your obliged and faithful Servt.
'J. Austen.'
'December 31, 1815.'

Chapter VIII

Slow growth of her fame—Ill success of first attempts at publication—Two Reviews of her works contrasted.

SELDOM HAS ANY LITERARY reputation been of such slow growth as that of Jane Austen. Readers of the present day know the rank that is generally assigned to her. They have been told by Archbishop Whately, in his review of her works, and by Lord Macaulay, in his review of Madame D'Arblay's, the reason why the highest place is to be awarded to Jane Austen, as a truthful drawer of character, and why she is to be classed with those who have approached nearest, in that respect, to the great master Shakespeare. They see her safely placed, by such authorities, in her niche, not indeed amongst the highest orders of genius, but in one confessedly her own, in our British temple of literary fame; and it may be difficult to make them believe how coldly her works were at first received, and how few readers had any appreciation of their peculiar merits. Sometimes a friend or neighbour, who chanced to know of our connection with the author, would condescend to speak with moderate approbation of *Sense and Sensibility*, or *Pride and Prejudice*; but if they had known that we, in our secret thoughts, classed her with Madame D'Arblay or Miss Edgeworth, or even with some other novel writers of the day whose names are now scarcely remembered, they would have considered it an amusing instance of family conceit. To the multitude her works appeared tame and commonplace,[57] poor in colouring, and sadly deficient in incident and interest. It is true that we were sometimes cheered by hearing that a different verdict had been pronounced by more competent judges: we were told how some great statesman or distinguished poet held these works in high estimation;

---

57 A greater genius than my aunt shared with her the imputation of being *commonplace*. Lockhart, speaking of the low estimation in which Scott's conversational powers were held in the literary and scientific society of Edinburgh, says: 'I think the epithet most in vogue concerning it was "commonplace."' He adds, however, that one of the most eminent of that society was of a different opinion, who, when some glib youth chanced to echo in his hearing the consolatory tenet of local mediocrity, answered quietly, "I have the misfortune to think differently from you—in my humble opinion Walter Scott's sense is a still more wonderful thing than his genius."—Lockhart's *Life of Scott*, vol. iv. chap. v.

we had the satisfaction of believing that they were most admired by the best judges, and comforted ourselves with Horace's 'satis est Equitem mihi plaudere.'[58] So much was this the case, that one of the ablest men of my acquaintance[59] said, in that kind of jest which has much earnest in it, that he had established it in his own mind, as a new test of ability, whether people *could* or *could not* appreciate Miss Austen's merits.

But though such golden opinions were now and then gathered in, yet the wide field of public taste yielded no adequate return either in praise or profit. Her reward was not to be the quick return of the cornfield, but the slow growth of the tree which is to endure to another generation. Her first attempts at publication were very discouraging. In November, 1797, her father wrote the following letter to Mr. Cadell:[60] —

'Sir,—I have in my possession a manuscript novel, comprising 3 vols., about the length of Miss Burney's *Evelina*.[61] As I am well aware of what consequence it is that a work of this sort shd make its first appearance under a respectable name, I apply to you. I shall be much obliged therefore if you will inform me whether you choose to be concerned in it, what will be the expense of publishing it at the author's risk, and what you will venture to advance for the property of it, if on perusal it is approved of. Should you give any encouragement, I will send you the work.

'I am, Sir, your humble Servant,

'George Austen.'

'Steventon, near Overton, Hants,

'1st Nov. 1797.'

This proposal was declined by return of post! The work thus summarily rejected must have been *Pride and Prejudice*.

The fate of *Northanger Abbey* was still more humiliating. It was sold, in 1803, to a publisher in Bath, for £10, but it found so little favour in

---

58 [The phrase is "*nam satis est equitem mihi plaudere*": "'Tis enough if the knights applaud me."]

59 The late Mr. R.H. Cheney.

60 [Thomas Cadell, 1742–1802, was an English bookseller and publisher.]

61 [Fanny Burney's *Evelina, or the History of a Young Lady's Entrance into the World*, published in 1778. Thought by some to be an influence on the work of Jane.]

his eyes, that he chose to abide by his first loss rather than risk farther expense by publishing such a work. It seems to have lain for many years unnoticed in his drawers; somewhat as the first chapters of *Waverley* lurked forgotten amongst the old fishing-tackle in Scott's cabinet. Tilneys, Thorpes, and Morlands consigned apparently to eternal oblivion! But when four novels of steadily increasing success had given the writer some confidence in herself, she wished to recover the copyright of this early work. One of her brothers undertook the negotiation. He found the purchaser very willing to receive back his money, and to resign all claim to the copyright. When the bargain was concluded and the money paid, but not till then, the negotiator had the satisfaction of informing him that the work which had been so lightly esteemed was by the author of *Pride and Prejudice*. I do not think that she was herself much mortified by the want of early success. She wrote for her own amusement. Money, though acceptable, was not necessary for the moderate expenses of her quiet home. Above all, she was blessed with a cheerful contented disposition, and an humble mind; and so lowly did she esteem her own claims, that when she received £150 from the sale of *Sense and Sensibility*, she considered it a prodigious recompense for that which had cost her nothing. It cannot be supposed, however, that she was altogether insensible to the superiority of her own workmanship over that of some contemporaries who were then enjoying a brief popularity. Indeed a few touches in the following extracts from two of her letters show that she was as quicksighted to absurdities in composition as to those in living persons.

'Mr. C.'s opinion is gone down in my list; but as my paper relates only to *Mansfield Park,* I may fortunately excuse myself from entering Mr. D's. I will redeem my credit with him by writing a close imitation of "Self-Control," as soon as I can. I will improve upon it. My heroine shall not only be wafted down an American river in a boat by herself. She shall cross the Atlantic in the same way; and never stop till she reaches Gravesend.'

'We have got *Rosanne* in our Society, and find it much as you describe it; very good and clever, but tedious. Mrs. Hawkins' [62] great excellence

---

62 [Laetitia Matilda Hawkins, *c.*1759–1835, was an English novelist and author of *Rosanne; or A father's labour lost*, published in 1814.]

is on serious subjects. There are some very delightful conversations and reflections on religion: but on lighter topics I think she falls into many absurdities; and, as to love, her heroine has very comical feelings. There are a thousand improbabilities in the story. Do you remember the two Miss Ormsdens introduced just at last? Very flat and unnatural. Madelle. Cossart is rather my passion.'

Two notices of her works appeared in the *Quarterly Review*. One in October 1815, and another, more than three years after her death, in January 1821. The latter article is known to have been from the pen of Whately, afterwards Archbishop of Dublin.[63] They differ much from each other in the degree of praise which they award, and I think also it may be said, in the ability with which they are written. The first bestows some approval, but the other expresses the warmest admiration. One can scarcely be satisfied with the critical acumen of the former writer, who, in treating of *Sense and Sensibility*, takes no notice whatever of the vigour with which many of the characters are drawn, but declares that 'the interest and *merit* of the piece depends *altogether* upon the behaviour of the elder sister!' Nor is he fair when, in *Pride and Prejudice,* he represents Elizabeth's change of sentiments towards Darcy as caused by the sight of his house and grounds. But the chief discrepancy between the two reviewers is to be found in their appreciation of the commonplace and silly characters to be found in these novels. On this point the difference almost amounts to a contradiction, such as one sometimes sees drawn up in parallel columns, when it is desired to convict some writer or some statesman of inconsistency. The Reviewer, in 1815, says: 'The faults of these works arise from the minute detail which the author's plan comprehends. Characters of folly or simplicity, such as those of old Woodhouse and Miss Bates, are ridiculous when first presented, but if too often brought forward, or too long dwelt on, their prosing is apt to become as tiresome in fic-

---

63 Lockhart had supposed that this article had been written by Scott, because it exactly accorded with the opinions which Scott had often been heard to express, but he learned afterwards that it had been written by Whately; and Lockhart, who became the Editor of the Quarterly, must have had the means of knowing the truth. (See Lockhart's *Life of Sir Walter Scott*, vol. v. p. 158.) I remember that, at the time when the review came out, it was reported in Oxford that Whately had written the article at the request of the lady whom he afterwards married.

tion as in real society.' The Reviewer, in 1821, on the contrary, singles out the fools as especial instances of the writer's abilities, and declares that in this respect she shows a regard to character hardly exceeded by Shakespeare himself. These are his words: 'Like him [Shakespeare] she shows as admirable a discrimination in the character of fools as of people of sense; a merit which is far from common. To invent indeed a conversation full of wisdom or of wit requires that the writer should himself possess ability; but the converse does not hold good, it is no fool that can describe fools well; and many who have succeeded pretty well in painting superior characters have failed in giving individuality to those weaker ones which it is necessary to introduce in order to give a faithful representation of real life: they exhibit to us mere folly in the abstract, forgetting that to the eye of the skilful naturalist the insects on a leaf present as wide differences as exist between the lion and the elephant. Slender, and Shallow, and Aguecheek, as Shakespeare has painted them, though equally fools, resemble one another no more than Richard, and Macbeth, and Julius Cæsar; and Miss Austen's[64] Mrs. Bennet, Mr. Rushworth, and Miss Bates are no more alike than her Darcy, Knightley, and Edmund Bertram. Some have complained indeed of finding her fools too much like nature, and consequently tiresome. There is no disputing about tastes; all we can say is, that such critics must (whatever deference they may outwardly pay to received opinions) find the *Merry Wives of Windsor* and *Twelfth Night* very tiresome; and that those who look with pleasure at Wilkie's pictures, or those of the Dutch school, must admit that excellence of imitation may confer attraction on that which would be insipid or disagreeable in the reality. Her minuteness of detail has also been found fault with; but even where it produces, at the time, a degree of tediousness, we know not whether that can justly be reckoned a blemish, which is absolutely essential to a very high excellence. Now it is absolutely impossible, without this, to produce that thorough acquaintance with the characters which is necessary to make the reader heartily interested in them. Let any one cut out from the *Iliad* or from Shakespeare's plays everything (we are far from saying that either might not lose some parts with advantage, but let him reject everything) which is absolutely devoid of

---

64 In transcribing this passage I have taken the liberty so far to correct it as to spell her name properly with an 'e.'

importance and interest *in itself*; and he will find that what is left will have lost more than half its charms. We are convinced that some writers have diminished the effect of their works by being scrupulous to admit nothing into them which had not some absolute and independent merit. They have acted like those who strip off the leaves of a fruit tree, as being of themselves good for nothing, with the view of securing more nourishment to the fruit, which in fact cannot attain its full maturity and flavour without them.'

The world, I think, has endorsed the opinion of the later writer; but it would not be fair to set down the discrepancy between the two entirely to the discredit of the former. The fact is that, in the course of the intervening five years, these works had been read and reread by many leaders in the literary world. The public taste was forming itself all this time, and 'grew by what it fed on.' These novels belong to a class which gain rather than lose by frequent perusals, and it is probable that each Reviewer represented fairly enough the prevailing opinions of readers in the year when each wrote.

Since that time, the testimonies in favour of Jane Austen's works have been continual and almost unanimous. They are frequently referred to as models; nor have they lost their first distinction of being especially acceptable to minds of the highest order. I shall indulge myself by collecting into the next chapter instances of the homage paid to her by such persons.

Chapter IX

Opinions expressed by eminent persons—Opinions of others
of less eminence—Opinion of American readers.

INTO THIS LIST OF the admirers of my Aunt's works, I admit those only whose eminence will be universally acknowledged. No doubt the number might have been increased.

Southey, in a letter to Sir Egerton Brydges, says: 'You mention Miss Austen. Her novels are more true to nature, and have, for my sympathies, passages of finer feeling than any others of this age. She was a person of whom I have heard so well and think so highly, that I regret not having had an opportunity of testifying to her the respect which I felt for her.'

It may be observed that Southey had probably heard from his own family connections of the charm of her private character. A friend of hers, the daughter of Mr. Bigge Wither, of Manydown Park near Basingstoke, was married to Southey's uncle, the Rev. Herbert Hill, who had been useful to his nephew in many ways, and especially in supplying him with the means of attaining his extensive knowledge of Spanish and Portuguese literature. Mr. Hill had been Chaplain to the British Factory at Lisbon, where Southey visited him and had the use of a library in those languages which his uncle had collected. Southey himself continually mentions his uncle Hill in terms of respect and gratitude.

S.T. Coleridge would sometimes burst out into high encomiums of Miss Austen's novels as being, 'in their way, perfectly genuine and individual productions.'

I remember Miss Mitford's saying to me: 'I would almost cut off one of my hands, if it would enable me to write like your aunt with the other.'

The biographer of Sir J. Mackintosh says: 'Something recalled to his mind the traits of character which are so delicately touched in Miss Austen's novels ... He said that there was genius in sketching out that new kind of novel ... He was vexed for the credit of the *Edinburgh Review* that it had left her unnoticed.[65] ... The *Quarterly* had done her

---

65 Incidentally she had received high praise in Lord Macaulay's Review of Madame D'Arblay's Works in the *Edinburgh*. [*Edinburgh Review* has been used for the title of four different magazines. This was probably the one than ran from 1802 to 1929 and that promoted Romanticism and liberal politics.]

more justice … It was impossible for a foreigner to understand fully the merit of her works. Madame de Staël,[66] to whom he had recommended one of her novels, found no interest in it; and in her note to him in reply said it was "vulgaire": and yet, he said, nothing could be more true than what he wrote in answer: "There is no book which that word would so little suit." … Every village could furnish matter for a novel to Miss Austen. She did not need the common materials for a novel, strong emotions, or strong incidents.'[67]

It was not, however, quite impossible for a foreigner to appreciate these works; for Mons. Guizot writes thus: 'I am a great novel reader, but I seldom read German or French novels. The characters are too artificial. My delight is to read English novels, particularly those written by women. "C'est toute une école de morale."[68] Miss Austen, Miss Ferrier, &c., form a school which in the excellence and profusion of its productions resembles the cloud of dramatic poets of the great Athenian age.'

In the *Keepsake* of 1825 the following lines appeared, written by Lord Morpeth, afterwards seventh Earl of Carlisle, and Lord-Lieutenant of Ireland, accompanying an illustration of a lady reading a novel.[69]

> Beats thy quick pulse o'er Inchbald's thrilling leaf,
> Brunton's high moral, Opie's deep wrought grief?
> Has the mild chaperon claimed thy yielding heart,
> Carroll's dark page, Trevelyan's gentle art?
> Or is it thou, all perfect Austen? Here
> Let one poor wreath adorn thy early bier,
> That scarce allowed thy modest youth to claim
> Its living portion of thy certain fame!
> Oh! Mrs. Bennet! Mrs. Norris too!
> While memory survives we'll dream of you.
> And Mr. Woodhouse, whose abstemious lip
> Must thin, but not too thin, his gruel sip.
> Miss Bates, our idol, though the village bore;
> And Mrs. Elton, ardent to explore.
> While the clear style flows on without pretence,

66 [Anne Louise Germaine de Staël-Holstein, 1766–1817, a Swiss-French woman influential in French politicss well as being a writer.]
67 *Life of Sir J. Mackintosh*, vol. ii. p. 472.
68 ['It is a whole school of morals.']
69 [The poem is called 'The Lady and the Novel'.]

With unstained purity, and unmatched sense:
Or, if a sister e'er approached the throne,
She called the rich 'inheritance' her own.

The admiration felt by Lord Macaulay would probably have taken a very practical form, if his life had been prolonged. I have the authority of his sister, Lady Trevelyan, for stating that he had intended to undertake the task upon which I have ventured. He purposed to write a memoir of Miss Austen, with criticisms on her works, to prefix it to a new edition of her novels, and from the proceeds of the sale to erect a monument to her memory in Winchester Cathedral. Oh! that such an idea had been realised! That portion of the plan in which Lord Macaulay's success would have been most certain might have been almost sufficient for his object. A memoir written by him would have been a monument.

I am kindly permitted by Sir Henry Holland to give the following quotation from his printed but unpublished recollections of his past life:—

'I have the picture still before me of Lord Holland lying on his bed, when attacked with gout, his admirable sister, Miss Fox, beside him reading aloud, as she always did on these occasions, some one of Miss Austen's novels, of which he was never wearied. I well recollect the time when these charming novels, almost unique in their style of humour, burst suddenly on the world. It was sad that their writer did not live to witness the growth of her fame.'

My brother-in-law, Sir Denis Le Marchant, has supplied me with the following anecdotes from his own recollections:—

'When I was a student at Trinity College, Cambridge, Mr. Whewell, then a Fellow and afterwards Master of the College, often spoke to me with admiration of Miss Austen's novels. On one occasion I said that I had found *Persuasion* rather dull. He quite fired up in defence of it, insisting that it was the most beautiful of her works. This accomplished philosopher was deeply versed in works of fiction. I recollect his writing to me from Caernarvon, where he had the charge of some pupils, that he was weary of *his* stay, for he had read the circulating library twice through.

'During a visit I paid to Lord Lansdowne, at Bowood, in 1846, one of Miss Austen's novels became the subject of conversation and of praise, especially from Lord Lansdowne, who observed that one of the circumstances of his life which he looked back upon with vexation was that Miss Austen should once have been living some weeks in his neighbourhood without his knowing it.

'I have heard Sydney Smith, more than once, dwell with eloquence on the merits of Miss Austen's novels. He told me he should have enjoyed giving her the pleasure of reading her praises in the *Edinburgh Review*. "Fanny Price" was one of his prime favourites.'

I close this list of testimonies, this long 'Catena Patrum,'[70] with the remarkable words of Sir Walter Scott, taken from his diary for March 14, 1826:[71] 'Read again, for the third time at least, Miss Austen's finely written novel of *Pride and Prejudice*. That young lady had a talent for describing the involvements and feelings and characters of ordinary life, which is to me the most wonderful I ever met with. The big Bow-Wow strain I can do myself like any now going; but the exquisite touch which renders ordinary common-place things and characters interesting from the truth of the description and the sentiment is denied to me. What a pity such a gifted creature died so early!' The well-worn condition of Scott's own copy of these works attests that they were much read in his family. When I visited Abbotsford, a few years after Scott's death, I was permitted, as an unusual favour, to take one of these volumes in my hands. One cannot suppress the wish that she had lived to know what such men thought of her powers, and how gladly they would have cultivated a personal acquaintance with her. I do not think that it would at all have impaired the modest simplicity of her character; or that we should have lost our own dear 'Aunt Jane' in the blaze of literary fame.

It may be amusing to contrast with these testimonies from the great, the opinions expressed by other readers of more ordinary intellect. The author herself has left a list of criticisms which it had been her amusement to collect, through means of her friends. This list contains much of warm-hearted sympathising praise, interspersed with some opinions which may be considered surprising.

---

70 ['Chain of the (Church) fathers'].
71 Lockhart's *Life of Scott*, vol. vi. chap. vii.

One lady could say nothing better of *Mansfield Park*, than that it was 'a mere novel.'

Another owned that she thought *Sense and Sensibility* and *Pride and Prejudice* downright nonsense; but expected to like *Mansfield Park* better, and having finished the first volume, hoped that she had got through the worst.

Another did not like *Mansfield Park*. Nothing interesting in the characters. Language poor.

One gentleman read the first and last chapters of *Emma*, but did not look at the rest because he had been told that it was not interesting.

The opinions of another gentleman about *Emma* were so bad that they could not be reported to the author.

'*Quot homines, tot sententiæ.*'[72]

Thirty-five years after her death there came also a voice of praise from across the Atlantic. In 1852 the following letter was received by her brother Sir Francis Austen:—

'Boston, Massachusetts, U.S.A.
6th Jan. 1852.

'Since high critical authority has pronounced the delineations of character in the works of Jane Austen second only to those of Shakespeare, transatlantic admiration appears superfluous; yet it may not be uninteresting to her family to receive an assurance that the influence of her genius is extensively recognised in the American Republic, even by the highest judicial authorities. The late Mr. Chief Justice Marshall, of the supreme Court of the United States, and his associate Mr. Justice Story, highly estimated and admired Miss Austen, and to them we owe our introduction to her society. For many years her talents have brightened our daily path, and her name and those of her characters are familiar to us as "household words." We have long wished to express to some of her family the sentiments of gratitude and affection she has inspired, and request more information relative to her life than is given in the brief memoir prefixed to her works.

'Having accidentally heard that a brother of Jane Austen held a high rank in the British Navy, we have obtained his address from our friend

---

72 ['So many men, so many opinions.']

Admiral Wormley, now resident in Boston, and we trust this expression of our feeling will be received by her relations with the kindness and urbanity characteristic of Admirals of *her creation*. Sir Francis Austen, or one of his family, would confer a great favour by complying with our request. The autograph of his sister, or a few lines in her handwriting, would be placed among our chief treasures.

'The family who delight in the companionship of Jane Austen, and who present this petition, are of English origin. Their ancestor held a high rank among the first emigrants to New England, and his name and character have been ably represented by his descendants in various public stations of trust and responsibility to the present time in the colony and state of Massachusetts. A letter addressed to Miss Quincey, care of the Honble Josiah Quincey, Boston, Massachusetts, would reach its destination.'

Sir Francis Austen returned a suitable reply to this application; and sent a long letter of his sister's, which, no doubt, still occupies the place of honour promised by the Quincey family.

Chapter X

Observations on the Novels.

IT IS NOT THE object of these memoirs to attempt a criticism on Jane Austen's novels. Those particulars only have been noticed which could be illustrated by the circumstances of her own life; but I now desire to offer a few observations on them, and especially on one point, on which my age renders me a competent witness—the fidelity with which they represent the opinions and manners of the class of society in which the author lived early in this century. They do this the more faithfully on account of the very deficiency with which they have been sometimes charged—namely, that they make no attempt to raise the standard of human life, but merely represent it as it was. They certainly were not written to support any theory or inculcate any particular moral, except indeed the great moral which is to be equally gathered from an observation of the course of actual life—namely, the superiority of high over low principles, and of greatness over littleness of mind. These writings are like photographs, in which no feature is softened; no ideal expression is introduced, all is the unadorned reflection of the natural object; and the value of such a faithful likeness must increase as time gradually works more and more changes in the face of society itself. A remarkable instance of this is to be found in her portraiture of the clergy. She was the daughter and the sister of clergymen, who certainly were not low specimens of their order: and she has chosen three of her heroes from that profession; but no one in these days can think that either Edmund Bertram or Henry Tilney had adequate ideas of the duties of a parish minister. Such, however, were the opinions and practice then prevalent among respectable and conscientious clergymen before their minds had been stirred, first by the Evangelical, and afterwards by the High Church movement which this century has witnessed. The country may be congratulated which, on looking back to such a fixed landmark, can find that it has been advancing instead of receding from it.

The long interval that elapsed between the completion of *Northanger Abbey* in 1798, and the commencement of *Mansfield Park* in 1811, may sufficiently account for any difference of style which may be perceived between her three earlier and her three later productions. If the former showed quite as much originality and genius, they may perhaps be thought to have less of the faultless finish and high polish which distinguish the latter. The characters of the John Dashwoods, Mr. Collins, and the Thorpes stand out from the canvas with a vigour and originality which cannot be surpassed; but I think that in her last three works are to be found a greater refinement of taste, a more nice sense of propriety, and a deeper insight into the delicate anatomy of the human heart, marking the difference between the brilliant girl and the mature woman. Far from being one of those who have over-written themselves, it may be affirmed that her fame would have stood on a narrower and less firm basis, if she had not lived to resume her pen at Chawton.

Some persons have surmised that she took her characters from individuals with whom she had been acquainted. They were so life-like that it was assumed that they must once have lived, and have been transferred bodily, as it were, into her pages. But surely such a supposition betrays an ignorance of the high prerogative of genius to create out of its own resources imaginary characters, who shall be true to nature and consistent in themselves. Perhaps, however, the distinction between keeping true to nature and servilely copying any one specimen of it is not always clearly apprehended. It is indeed true, both of the writer and of the painter, that he can use only such lineaments as exist, and as he has observed to exist, in living objects; otherwise he would produce monsters instead of human beings; but in both it is the office of high art to mould these features into new combinations, and to place them in the attitudes, and impart to them the expressions which may suit the purposes of the artist; so that they are nature, but not exactly the same nature which had come before his eyes; just as honey can be obtained only from the natural flowers which the bee has sucked; yet it is not a reproduction of the odour or flavour of any particular flower, but becomes something different when it has gone through the process of transformation which that little insect is able to effect. Hence, in the case of painters, arises the superiority of original compositions over portrait painting. Reynolds was exercising a higher faculty when he designed Comedy and Tragedy contending for Garrick, than when he merely took a likeness of that actor. The same difference exists in writings between the original conceptions of Shakespeare and some other creative geniuses, and such full-length likenesses of individual persons, 'The Talking Gentleman' for instance, as are admirably drawn by Miss Mitford. Jane Austen's powers, whatever may be the degree in which she possessed them, were certainly of that higher order. She did not copy individuals, but she invested her own creations with individuality of character. A reviewer in the *Quarterly* speaks of an acquaintance who, ever since the publication of *Pride and Prejudice*, had been called by his friends Mr. Bennet, but the author did not know him. Her own relations never recognised any individual in her characters; and I can call to mind several of her acquaintance whose peculiarities were very tempting and easy to be caricatured of whom there are no traces in her pages. She herself, when questioned on the subject by a friend, expressed a dread of what she called such an 'invasion of social proprieties.' She said that she thought it quite fair to note peculiarities and weaknesses, but that it was her desire to create, not to reproduce; 'besides,' she added, 'I am too proud of my gentlemen to admit that they were only Mr. A. or Colonel B.' She did not, however, suppose that her imaginary characters were of a higher order than are to be found in nature; for she said, when speaking of two of her great favourites, Edmund Bertram and Mr. Knightley: 'They are very far from being what I know English gentlemen often are.'

She certainly took a kind of parental interest in the beings whom she had created, and did not dismiss them from her thoughts when she had finished her last chapter. We have seen, in one of her letters, her personal affection for Darcy and Elizabeth; and when sending a copy of *Emma* to a friend whose daughter had been lately born, she wrote thus: 'I trust you will be as glad to see my *Emma*, as I shall be to see your Jemima.' She was very fond of *Emma*, but did not reckon on her being a general favourite; for, when commencing that work, she said, 'I am going to take a heroine whom no one but myself will much like.' She would, if asked, tell us many little particulars about the subsequent career of some of her people. In this traditionary way we learned that Miss Steele never succeeded in catching the Doctor; that Kitty Bennet was satisfactorily married to a clergyman near Pemberley, while Mary obtained nothing higher than one of her uncle Philip's clerks, and was content to be considered a star in the society of Meriton; that the 'considerable sum' given by Mrs. Norris to William Price was one pound; that Mr. Woodhouse survived his daughter's marriage, and kept her and Mr. Knightley from settling at Donwell, about two years; and that the letters placed by Frank Churchill before Jane Fairfax, which she swept away unread, contained the word 'pardon.' Of the good people in *Northanger Abbey* and *Persuasion* we know nothing more than what is written: for before those works were published their author had been taken away from us, and all such amusing communications had ceased for ever.

Chapter XI

Declining health of Jane Austen—Elasticity of her spirits—
Her resignation and humility—Her death.

EARLY IN THE YEAR 1816 some family troubles disturbed the usually tranquil course of Jane Austen's life; and it is probable that the
inward malady, which was to prove ultimately fatal, was already felt by
her; for some distant friends,[73] whom she visited in the spring of that
year, thought that her health was somewhat impaired, and observed
that she went about her old haunts, and recalled old recollections connected with them in a particular manner, as if she did not expect ever
to see them again. It is not surprising that, under these circumstances,
some of her letters were of a graver tone than had been customary with
her, and expressed resignation rather than cheerfulness. In reference
to these troubles in a letter to her brother Charles, after mentioning
that she had been laid up with an attack of bilious fever, she says: 'I
live up stairs for the present and am coddled. I am the only one of the
party who has been so silly, but a weak body must excuse weak nerves.'
And again, to another correspondent: 'But I am getting too near complaint; it has been the appointment of God, however secondary causes
may have operated.' But the elasticity of her spirits soon recovered their
tone. It was in the latter half of that year that she addressed the two
following lively letters to a nephew, one while he was at Winchester
School, the other soon after he had left it:—

'Chawton, July 9, 1816.
    'My Dear E.—Many thanks. A thank for every line, and as many to
Mr. W. Digweed for coming. We have been wanting very much to hear
of your mother, and are happy to find she continues to mend, but her
illness must have been a very serious one indeed. When she is really
recovered, she ought to try change of air, and come over to us. Tell your
father that I am very much obliged to him for his share of your letter,
and most sincerely join in the hope of her being eventually much the
better for her present discipline. She has the comfort moreover of being

---

73 The Fowles, of Kintbury, in Berkshire.

confined in such weather as gives one little temptation to be out. It is really too bad, and has been too bad for a long time, much worse than any one can bear, and I begin to think it will never be fine again. This is a *finesse* of mine, for I have often observed that if one writes about the weather, it is generally completely changed before the letter is read. I wish it may prove so now, and that when Mr. W. Digweed reaches Steventon to-morrow, he may find you have had a long series of hot dry weather. We are a small party at present, only grandmamma, Mary Jane, and myself. Yalden's coach cleared off the rest yesterday. I am glad you recollected to mention your being come home.[74] My heart began to sink within me when I had got so far through your letter without its being mentioned. I was dreadfully afraid that you might be detained at Winchester by severe illness, confined to your bed perhaps, and quite unable to hold a pen, and only dating from Steventon in order, with a mistaken sort of tenderness, to deceive me. But now I have no doubt of your being at home. I am sure you would not say it so seriously unless it actually were so. We saw a countless number of post-chaises full of boys pass by yesterday morning[75]—full of future heroes, legislators, fools, and villains. You have never thanked me for my last letter, which went by the cheese. I cannot bear not to be thanked. You will not pay us a visit yet of course; we must not think of it. Your mother must get well first, and you must go to Oxford and *not* be elected; after that a little change of scene may be good for you, and your physicians I hope will order you to the sea, or to a house by the side of a very considerable pond.[76] Oh! it rains again. It beats against the window. Mary Jane and I have been wet through once already to-day; we set off in the donkey-carriage for Farringdon, as I wanted to see the improvement Mr. Woolls is making, but we were obliged to turn back before we got there, but not soon enough to avoid a pelter all the way home. We met Mr. Woolls. I talked of its being bad weather for the hay, and he returned me the comfort of its being much worse for the wheat.

---

74 It seems that her young correspondent, after dating from his home, had been so superfluous as to state in his letter that he was returned home, and thus to have drawn on himself this banter.

75 The road by which many Winchester boys returned home ran close to Chawton Cottage.

76 There was, though it exists no longer, a pond close to Chawton Cottage, at the junction of the Winchester and Gosport roads.

We hear that Mrs. S. does not quit Tangier: why and wherefore? Do you know that our Browning is gone? You must prepare for a William when you come, a good-looking lad, civil and quiet, and seeming likely to do. Good bye. I am sure Mr. W.D.[77] will be astonished at my writing so much, for the paper is so thin that he will be able to count the lines if not to read them.

Yours affec[ly],

'Jane Austen.'

In the next letter will be found her description of her own style of composition, which has already appeared in the notice prefixed to *Northanger Abbey* and *Persuasion*:—

'Chawton, Monday, Dec. 16th (1816).

'My Dear E.,—One reason for my writing to you now is, that I may have the pleasure of directing to you Esq[re]. I give you joy of having left Winchester. Now you may own how miserable you were there; now it will gradually all come out, your crimes and your miseries—how often you went up by the Mail to London and threw away fifty guineas at a tavern, and how often you were on the point of hanging yourself, restrained only, as some ill-natured aspersion upon poor old Winton has it, by the want of a tree within some miles of the city. Charles Knight and his companions passed through Chawton about 9 this morning; later than it used to be. Uncle Henry and I had a glimpse of his handsome face, looking all health and good humour. I wonder when you will come and see us. I know what I rather speculate upon, but shall say nothing. We think uncle Henry in excellent looks. Look at him this moment, and think so too, if you have not done it before; and we have the great comfort of seeing decided improvement in uncle Charles, both as to health, spirits, and appearance. And they are each of them so agreeable in their different way, and harmonise so well, that their visit is thorough enjoyment. Uncle Henry writes very superior sermons. You and I must try to get hold of one or two, and put them into our novels: it would be a fine help to a volume; and we could make our heroine read it aloud on a Sunday evening, just as well as Isabella

---

77 Mr. Digweed, who conveyed the letters to and from Chawton, was the gentleman named earlier, as renting the old manor-house and the large farm at Steventon.

Wardour, in the *Antiquary*,[78] is made to read the *History of the Hartz Demon* in the ruins of St. Ruth, though I believe, on recollection, Lovell is the reader. By the bye, my dear E., I am quite concerned for the loss your mother mentions in her letter. Two chapters and a half to be missing is monstrous! It is well that *I* have not been at Steventon lately, and therefore cannot be suspected of purloining them: two strong twigs and a half towards a nest of my own would have been something. I do not think, however, that any theft of that sort would be really very useful to me. What should I do with your strong, manly, vigorous sketches, full of variety and glow? How could I possibly join them on to the little bit (two inches wide) of ivory on which I work with so fine a brush, as produces little effect after much labour?

'You will hear from uncle Henry how well Anna is. She seems perfectly recovered. Ben was here on Saturday, to ask uncle Charles and me to dine with them, as to-morrow, but I was forced to decline it, the walk is beyond my strength (though I am otherwise very well), and this is not a season for donkey-carriages; and as we do not like to spare uncle Charles, he has declined it too.

Tuesday. Ah, ah! Mr. E. I doubt your seeing uncle Henry at Steventon to-day. The weather will prevent your expecting him, I think. Tell your father, with aunt Cass's love and mine, that the pickled cucumbers are extremely good, and tell him also—"tell him what you will." No, don't tell him what you will, but tell him that grandmamma begs him to make Joseph Hall pay his rent, if he can.

'You must not be tired of reading the word *uncle*, for I have not done with it. Uncle Charles thanks your mother for her letter; it was a great pleasure to him to know that the parcel was received and gave so much satisfaction, and he begs her to be so good as to give three shillings for him to Dame Staples, which shall be allowed for in the payment of her debt here.

'Adieu, Amiable! I hope Caroline behaves well to you.

Yours affec.ly,

'J. Austen.'

---

78 [*The Antiquary* by Sir Walter Scott, 1771–1832, a Scottish writer.]

I cannot tell how soon she was aware of the serious nature of her malady. By God's mercy it was not attended with much suffering; so that she was able to tell her friends as in the foregoing letter, and perhaps sometimes to persuade herself that, excepting want of strength, she was 'otherwise very well;' but the progress of the disease became more and more manifest as the year advanced. The usual walk was at first shortened, and then discontinued; and air was sought in a donkey-carriage. Gradually, too, her habits of activity within the house ceased, and she was obliged to lie down much. The sitting-room contained only one sofa, which was frequently occupied by her mother, who was more than seventy years old. Jane would never use it, even in her mother's absence; but she contrived a sort of couch for herself with two or three chairs, and was pleased to say that this arrangement was more comfortable to her than a real sofa. Her reasons for this might have been left to be guessed, but for the importunities of a little niece, which obliged her to explain that if she herself had shown any inclination to use the sofa, her mother might have scrupled being on it so much as was good for her.

It is certain, however, that the mind did not share in this decay of the bodily strength. *Persuasion* was not finished before the middle of August in that year; and the manner in which it was then completed affords proof that neither the critical nor the creative powers of the author were at all impaired. The book had been brought to an end in July; and the re-engagement of the hero and heroine effected in a totally different manner in a scene laid at Admiral Croft's lodgings. But her performance did not satisfy her. She thought it tame and flat, and was desirous of producing something better. This weighed upon her mind, the more so probably on account of the weak state of her health; so that one night she retired to rest in very low spirits. But such depression was little in accordance with her nature, and was soon shaken off. The next morning she awoke to more cheerful views and brighter inspirations: the sense of power revived; and imagination resumed its course. She cancelled the condemned chapter, and wrote two others, entirely different, in its stead. The result is that we possess the visit of the Musgrove party to Bath; the crowded and animated scenes at the White Hart Hotel; and the charming conversation between Capt. Harville and Anne Elliot, overheard by Capt. Wentworth, by which the two faithful lovers were at last led to understand each other's feelings. The tenth and eleventh chapters of *Persuasion* then, rather than the actual winding-up of the story, contain the latest of her printed compositions, her last contribution to the entertainment of the public. Perhaps it may be thought that she has seldom written anything more brilliant; and that, independent of the original manner in which the *dénouement* is brought about, the pictures of Charles Musgrove's good-natured boyishness and of his wife's jealous selfishness would have been incomplete without these finishing strokes. The cancelled chapter exists in manuscript. It is certainly inferior to the two which were substituted for it: but it was such as some writers and some readers might have been contented with; and it contained touches which scarcely any other hand could have given, the suppression of which may be almost a matter of regret.

The following letter was addressed to her friend Miss Bigg, then staying at Streatham with her sister, the wife of the Reverend Herbert Hill, uncle of Robert Southey. It appears to have been written three days before she began her last work, which will be noticed in another chapter; and shows that she was not at that time aware of the serious nature of her malady:—

'Chawton, January 24, 1817.

'My Dear Alethea,—I think it time there should be a little writing between us, though I believe the epistolary debt is on *your* side, and I hope this will find all the Streatham party well, neither carried away by the flood, nor rheumatic through the damps. Such mild weather is, you know, delightful to *us*, and though we have a great many ponds, and a fine running stream through the meadows on the other side of the road, it is nothing but what beautifies us and does to talk of. *I* have certainly gained strength through the winter and am not far from being well; and I think I understand my own case now so much better than I did, as to be able by care to keep off any serious return of illness. I am convinced that *bile* is at the bottom of all I have suffered, which makes it easy to know how to treat myself. You will be glad to hear thus much of me, I am sure. We have just had a few days' visit from Edward, who brought us a good account of his father, and the very circumstance of his coming at all, of his father's being able to spare him, is itself a good account. He grows still, and still improves in appearance, at least in the estimation of his aunts, who love him better and better, as they see the sweet temper and warm affections of the boy confirmed in the young man: I tried hard to persuade him that he must have some message for William,[79] but in vain ... This is not a time of year for donkey-carriages, and our donkeys are necessarily having so long a run of luxurious idleness that I suppose we shall find they have forgotten much of their education when we use them again. We do not use two at once however; don't imagine such excesses ... Our own new clergyman[80] is expected here very soon, perhaps in time to assist Mr. Papillon on Sunday. I shall be very glad when the first hearing is over. It will be a nervous hour for our pew, though we hear that he acquits himself with as much ease and collectedness, as if he had been used to it all his life. We have no chance we know of seeing you between Streatham and Winchester: you go the other road and are engaged to two or three houses; if there should be any change, however, you know how welcome you would be ... We have been reading the *Poet's Pilgrimage to Waterloo*,[81] and generally with much approbation. Nothing will please all the world, you know; but parts of it suit me better than much that he has written before. The opening—*the proem* I believe he calls it—is very beautiful. Poor man! one cannot but grieve for the loss of the son so fondly described. Has he at all recovered it? What do Mr. and Mrs. Hill know about his present state?

'Yours aff[ly],

J. Austen.

'The real object of this letter is to ask you for a receipt, but I thought it genteel not to let it appear early. We remember some excellent orange wine at Manydown, made from Seville oranges, entirely or chiefly. I should be very much obliged to you for the receipt, if you can command it within a few weeks.'

On the day before, January 23rd, she had written to her niece in the same hopeful tone: 'I feel myself getting stronger than I was, and can so perfectly walk *to* Alton, *or* back again without fatigue, that I hope to be able to do *both* when summer comes.'

---

79 Miss Bigg's nephew, the present Sir William Heathcote, of Hursley.
80 Her brother Henry, who had been ordained late in life.
81 [By Robert Southey and published in 1816.]

Alas! summer came to her only on her deathbed. March 17th is the last date to be found in the manuscript on which she was engaged; and as the watch of the drowned man indicates the time of his death, so does this final date seem to fix the period when her mind could no longer pursue its accustomed course.

And here I cannot do better than quote the words of the niece to whose private records of her aunt's life and character I have been so often indebted:—

'I do not know how early the alarming symptoms of her malady came on. It was in the following March that I had the first idea of her being seriously ill. It had been settled that about the end of that month, or the beginning of April, I should spend a few days at Chawton, in the absence of my father and mother, who were just then engaged with Mrs. Leigh Perrot in arranging her late husband's affairs; but Aunt Jane became too ill to have me in the house, and so I went instead to my sister Mrs. Lefroy at Wyards'. The next day we walked over to Chawton to make enquiries after our aunt. She was then keeping her room, but said she would see us, and we went up to her. She was in her dressing gown, and was sitting quite like an invalid in an arm-chair, but she got up and kindly greeted us, and then, pointing to seats which had been arranged for us by the fire, she said, "There is a chair for the married lady, and a little stool for you, Caroline." [82] It is strange, but those trifling words were the last of hers that I can remember, for I retain no recollection of what was said by anyone in the conversation that ensued. I was struck by the alteration in herself. She was very pale, her voice was weak and low, and there was about her a general appearance of debility and suffering; but I have been told that she never had much acute pain. She was not equal to the exertion of talking to us, and our visit to the sick room was a very short one, Aunt Cassandra soon taking us away. I do not suppose we stayed a quarter of an hour; and I never saw Aunt Jane again.'

In May 1817 she was persuaded to remove to Winchester, for the sake of medical advice from Mr. Lyford. The Lyfords have, for some generations, maintained a high character in Winchester for medical skill, and the Mr. Lyford of that day was a man of more than provincial

---

82 The writer was at that time under twelve years old.

reputation, in whom great London practitioners expressed confidence. Mr. Lyford spoke encouragingly. It was not, of course, his business to extinguish hope in his patient, but I believe that he had, from the first, very little expectation of a permanent cure. All that was gained by the removal from home was the satisfaction of having done the best that could be done, together with such alleviations of suffering as superior medical skill could afford.

Jane and her sister Cassandra took lodgings in College Street. They had two kind friends living in the Close, Mrs. Heathcote and Miss Bigg, the mother and aunt of the present Sir Wm. Heathcote of Hursley, between whose family and ours a close friendship has existed for several generations. These friends did all that they could to promote the comfort of the sisters, during that sad sojourn in Winchester, both by their society, and by supplying those little conveniences in which a lodging-house was likely to be deficient. It was shortly after settling in these lodgings that she wrote to a nephew the following characteristic letter, no longer, alas in her former strong, clear hand.

'Mrs. David's, College St., Winton,
'Tuesday, May 27th.

'There is no better way, my dearest E., of thanking you for your affectionate concern for me during my illness than by telling you myself, as soon as possible, that I continue to get better. I will not boast of my handwriting; neither that nor my face have yet recovered their proper beauty, but in other respects I gain strength very fast. I am now out of bed from 9 in the morning to 10 at night: upon the sofa, it is true, but I eat my meals with aunt Cassandra in a rational way, and can employ myself, and walk from one room to another. Mr. Lyford says he will cure me, and if he fails, I shall draw up a memorial and lay it before the Dean and Chapter, and have no doubt of redress from that pious, learned, and disinterested body. Our lodgings are very comfortable. We have a neat little drawing-room with a bow window overlooking Dr. Gabell's garden.[83] Thanks to the kindness of your father and mother in sending me their carriage, my journey hither on Saturday was performed with very little fatigue, and had it been a fine day, I think I

---

83 It was the corner house in College Street, at the entrance to Commoners.

should have felt none; but it distressed me to see uncle Henry and Wm. Knight, who kindly attended us on horseback, riding in the rain almost the whole way. We expect a visit from them to-morrow, and hope they will stay the night; and on Thursday, which is a confirmation and a holiday, we are to get Charles out to breakfast. We have had but one visit from *him*, poor fellow, as he is in sick-room, but he hopes to be out to-night. We see Mrs. Heathcote every day, and William is to call upon us soon. God bless you, my dear E. If ever you are ill, may you be as tenderly nursed as I have been. May the same blessed alleviations of anxious, sympathising friends be yours: and may you possess, as I dare say you will, the greatest blessing of all in the consciousness of not being unworthy of their love. *I* could not feel this.

'Your very affec^te Aunt,

'J.A.'

The following extract from a letter which has been before printed, written soon after the former, breathes the same spirit of humility and thankfulness:—

'I will only say further that my dearest sister, my tender, watchful, indefatigable nurse, has not been made ill by her exertions. As to what I owe her, and the anxious affection of all my beloved family on this occasion, I can only cry over it, and pray God to bless them more and more.'

Throughout her illness she was nursed by her sister, often assisted by her sister-in-law, my mother. Both were with her when she died. Two of her brothers, who were clergymen, lived near enough to Winchester to be in frequent attendance, and to administer the services suitable for a Christian's death-bed. While she used the language of hope to her correspondents, she was fully aware of her danger, though not appalled by it. It is true that there was much to attach her to life. She was happy in her family; she was just beginning to feel confidence in her own success; and, no doubt, the exercise of her great talents was an enjoyment in itself. We may well believe that she would gladly have lived longer; but she was enabled without dismay or complaint to prepare for death. She was a humble, believing Christian. Her life had been passed in the performance of home duties, and the cultivation of domestic affections, without any self-seeking or craving after applause. She had always sought, as it were by instinct, to promote the happiness of all who came within her influence, and doubtless she had her reward in the peace of mind which was granted her in her last days. Her sweetness of temper never failed. She was ever considerate and grateful to those who attended on her. At times, when she felt rather better, her playfulness of spirit revived, and she amused them even in their sadness. Once, when she thought herself near her end, she said what she imagined might be her last words to those around her, and particularly thanked her sister-in-law for being with her, saying: 'You have always been a kind sister to me, Mary.' When the end at last came, she sank rapidly, and on being asked by her attendants whether there was anything that she wanted, her reply was, '*Nothing but death.*' These were her last words. In quietness and peace she breathed her last on the morning of July 18, 1817.

On the 24th of that month she was buried in Winchester Cathedral, near the centre of the north aisle, almost opposite to the beautiful chantry tomb of William of Wykeham. A large slab of black marble in the pavement marks the place. Her own family only attended the funeral. Her sister returned to her desolated home, there to devote herself, for ten years, to the care of her aged mother; and to live much on the memory of her lost sister, till called many years later to rejoin her. Her brothers went back sorrowing to their several homes. They were very fond and very proud of her. They were attached to her by her talents, her virtues, and her engaging manners; and each loved afterwards to fancy a resemblance in some niece or daughter of his own to the dear sister Jane, whose perfect equal they yet never expected to see.

Chapter XII

The Cancelled Chapter (Chap. X.) of Persuasion.

WITH ALL THIS KNOWLEDGE of Mr. Elliot and this authority to impart it, Anne left Westgate Buildings, her mind deeply busy in revolving what she had heard, feeling, thinking, recalling, and foreseeing everything, shocked at Mr. Elliot, sighing over future Kellynch, and pained for Lady Russell, whose confidence in him had been entire. The embarrassment which must be felt from this hour in his presence! How to behave to him? How to get rid of him? What to do by any of the party at home? Where to be blind? Where to be active? It was altogether a confusion of images and doubts—a perplexity, an agitation which she could not see the end of. And she was in Gay Street, and still so much engrossed that she started on being addressed by Admiral Croft, as if he were a person unlikely to be met there. It was within a few steps of his own door.

'You are going to call upon my wife,' said he. 'She will be very glad to see you.'

Anne denied it.

'No! she really had not time, she was in her way home;' but while she spoke the Admiral had stepped back and knocked at the door, calling out,

'Yes, yes; do go in; she is all alone; go in and rest yourself.'

Anne felt so little disposed at this time to be in company of any sort, that it vexed her to be thus constrained, but she was obliged to stop.

'Since you are so very kind,' said she, 'I will just ask Mrs. Croft how she does, but I really cannot stay five minutes. You are sure she is quite alone?'

The possibility of Captain Wentworth had occurred; and most fearfully anxious was she to be assured—either that he was within, or that he was not—*which* might have been a question.

'Oh yes! quite alone, nobody but her mantua-maker with her, and they have been shut up together this half-hour, so it must be over soon.'

'Her mantua-maker! Then I am sure my calling now would be most inconvenient. Indeed you must allow me to leave my card and be so good as to explain it afterwards to Mrs. Croft.'

'No, no, not at all—not at all—she will be very happy to see you. Mind, I will not swear that she has not something particular to say to you, but that will all come out in the right place. I give no hints. Why, Miss Elliot, we begin to hear strange things of you (smiling in her face). But you have not much the look of it, as grave as a little judge!'

Anne blushed.

'Aye, aye, that will do now, it is all right. I thought we were not mistaken.'

She was left to guess at the direction of his suspicions; the first wild idea had been of some disclosure from his brother-in-law, but she was ashamed the next moment, and felt how far more probable it was that he should be meaning Mr. Elliot. The door was opened, and the man evidently beginning to *deny* his mistress, when the sight of his master stopped him. The Admiral enjoyed the joke exceedingly. Anne thought his triumph over Stephen rather too long. At last, however, he was able to invite her up stairs, and stepping before her said, 'I will just go up with you myself and show you in. I cannot stay, because I must go to the Post-Office, but if you will only sit down for five minutes I am sure Sophy will come, and you will find nobody to disturb you—there is nobody but Frederick here,' opening the door as he spoke. Such a person to be passed over as nobody to *her*! After being allowed to feel quite secure, indifferent, at her ease, to have it burst on her that she was to be the next moment in the same room with him! No time for recollection! for planning behaviour or regulating manners! There was time only to turn pale before she had passed through the door, and met the astonished eyes of Captain Wentworth, who was sitting by the fire, pretending to read, and prepared for no greater surprise than the Admiral's hasty return.

Equally unexpected was the meeting on each side. There was nothing to be done, however, but to stifle feelings, and to be quietly polite, and the Admiral was too much on the alert to leave any troublesome pause. He repeated again what he had said before about his wife and everybody, insisted on Anne's sitting down and being perfectly comfortable—was sorry he must leave her himself, but was sure Mrs. Croft would be down very soon, and would go upstairs and give her notice directly. Anne *was* sitting down, but now she arose, again to entreat him not to interrupt Mrs. Croft and re-urge the wish of going away and calling another time. But the Admiral would not hear of it; and if she did not return to the charge with unconquerable perseverance, or did not with a more passive determination walk quietly out of the room (as certainly she might have done), may she not be pardoned? If she *had* no horror of a few minutes' tête-à-tête with Captain Wentworth, may she not be pardoned for not wishing to give him the idea that she had? She reseated herself, and the Admiral took leave, but on reaching the door, said—

'Frederick, a word with *you* if you please.'

Captain Wentworth went to him, and instantly, before they were well out of the room, the Admiral continued—

'As I am going to leave you together, it is but fair I should give you something to talk of; and so, if you please—'

Here the door was very firmly closed, she could guess by which of the two—and she lost entirely what immediately followed, but it was impossible for her not to distinguish parts of the rest, for the Admiral, on the strength of the door's being shut, was speaking without any management of voice, though she could hear his companion trying to check him. She could not doubt their being speaking of her. She heard her own name and Kellynch repeatedly. She was very much disturbed. She knew not what to do, or what to expect, and among other agonies felt the possibility of Captain Wentworth's not returning into the room at all, which, after her consenting to stay, would have been—too bad for language. They seemed to be talking of the Admiral's lease of Kellynch. She heard him say something of the lease being signed—or not signed—*that* was not likely to be a very agitating subject, but then followed—

'I hate to be at an uncertainty. I must know at once. Sophy thinks the same.'

Then in a lower tone Captain Wentworth seemed remonstrating, wanting to be excused, wanting to put something off.

'Phoo, phoo,' answered the Admiral, 'now is the time; if you will not speak, I will stop and speak myself.'

'Very well, sir, very well, sir,' followed with some impatience from his companion, opening the door as he spoke—

'You will then, you promise you will?' replied the Admiral in all the power of his natural voice, unbroken even by one thin door.

'Yes, sir, yes.' And the Admiral was hastily left, the door was closed, and the moment arrived in which Anne was alone with Captain Wentworth.

She could not attempt to see how he looked, but he walked immediately to a window as if irresolute and embarrassed, and for about the space of five seconds she repented what she had done—censured it as unwise, blushed over it as indelicate. She longed to be able to speak of the weather or the concert, but could only compass the relief of taking a newspaper in her hand. The distressing pause was over, however; he turned round in half a minute, and coming towards the table where she sat, said in a voice of effort and constraint—

'You must have heard too much already, Madam, to be in any doubt of my having promised Admiral Croft to speak to you on a particular subject, and this conviction determines me to do so, however repugnant to my—to all my sense of propriety to be taking so great a liberty! You will acquit me of impertinence I trust, by considering me as speaking only for another, and speaking by necessity; and the Admiral is a man who can never be thought impertinent by one who knows him as you do. His intentions are always the kindest and the best, and you will perceive he is actuated by none other in the application which I am now, with—with very peculiar feelings—obliged to make.' He stopped, but merely to recover breath, not seeming to expect any answer. Anne listened as if her life depended on the issue of his speech. He proceeded with a forced alacrity:—

'The Admiral, Madam, was this morning confidently informed that you were—upon my soul, I am quite at a loss, ashamed (breathing and speaking quickly)—the awkwardness of *giving* information of this kind to one of the parties—you can be at no loss to understand me. It was very confidently said that Mr. Elliot—that everything was settled in the family for a union between Mr. Elliot and yourself. It was added that you were to live at Kellynch—that Kellynch was to be given up. This the Admiral knew could not be correct. But it occurred to him that it might be the *wish* of the parties. And my commission from him, Madam, is to say, that if the family wish is such, his lease of Kellynch shall be cancelled, and he and my sister will provide themselves with another home, without imagining themselves to be doing anything which under similar circumstances would not be done for *them*. This is all, Madam. A very few words in reply from you will be sufficient. That

I should be the person commissioned on this subject is extraordinary! and believe me, Madam, it is no less painful. A very few words, however, will put an end to the awkwardness and distress we may *both* be feeling.'

Anne spoke a word or two, but they were unintelligible; and before she could command herself, he added, 'If you will only tell me that the Admiral may address a line to Sir Walter, it will be enough. Pronounce only the words, *he may*, and I shall immediately follow him with your message.'

'No, Sir,' said Anne; 'there is no message. You are misin—the Admiral is misinformed. I do justice to the kindness of his intentions, but he is quite mistaken. There is no truth in any such report.'

He was a moment silent. She turned her eyes towards him for the first time since his re-entering the room. His colour was varying, and he was looking at her with all the power and keenness which she believed no other eyes than his possessed.

'No truth in any such report?' he repeated. 'No truth in any *part* of it?'

'None.'

He had been standing by a chair, enjoying the relief of leaning on it, or of playing with it. He now sat down, drew it a little nearer to her, and looked with an expression which had something more than penetration in it—something softer. Her countenance did not discourage. It was a silent but a very powerful dialogue; on his supplication, on hers acceptance. Still a little nearer, and a hand taken and pressed; and 'Anne, my own dear Anne!' bursting forth in all the fulness of exquisite feeling,—and all suspense and indecision were over. They were re-united. They were restored to all that had been lost. They were carried back to the past with only an increase of attachment and confidence, and only such a flutter of present delight as made them little fit for the interruption of Mrs. Croft when she joined them not long afterwards. *She*, probably, in the observations of the next ten minutes saw something to suspect; and though it was hardly possible for a woman of her description to wish the mantua-maker had imprisoned her longer, she might be very likely wishing for some excuse to run about the house, some storm to break the windows above, or a summons to the Admiral's shoemaker below. Fortune favoured them all, however, in another way, in a gentle, steady rain, just happily set in as the Admiral returned and

Anne rose to go. She was earnestly invited to stay dinner. A note was despatched to Camden Place, and she staid—staid till ten at night; and during that time the husband and wife, either by the wife's contrivance, or by simply going on in their usual way, were frequently out of the room together—gone upstairs to hear a noise, or downstairs to settle their accounts, or upon the landing to trim the lamp. And these precious moments were turned to so good an account that all the most anxious feelings of the past were gone through. Before they parted at night, Anne had the felicity of being assured that in the first place (so far from being altered for the worse), she had gained inexpressibly in personal loveliness; and that as to character, hers was now fixed on his mind as *perfection* itself, maintaining the just medium of fortitude and gentleness—that he had never ceased to love and prefer her, though it had been only at Uppercross that he had learnt to do her justice, and only at Lyme that he had begun to understand his own feelings; that at Lyme he had received lessons of more than one kind—the passing admiration of Mr. Elliot had at least *roused* him, and the scene on the Cobb, and at Captain Harville's, had fixed her superiority. In his preceding attempts to attach himself to Louisa Musgrove (the attempts of anger and pique), he protested that he had continually felt the impossibility of really caring for Louisa, though till *that day*, till the leisure for reflection which followed it, he had not understood the perfect excellence of the mind with which Louisa's could so ill bear comparison; or the perfect, the unrivalled hold it possessed over his own. There he had learnt to distinguish between the steadiness of principle and the obstinacy of self-will, between the darings of heedlessness and the resolution of a collected mind; there he had seen everything to exalt in his estimation the woman he had lost, and there had begun to deplore the pride, the folly, the madness of resentment, which had kept him from trying to regain her when thrown in his way. From that period to the present had his penance been the most severe. He had no sooner been free from the horror and remorse attending the first few days of Louisa's accident, no sooner had begun to feel himself alive again, than he had begun to feel himself, though alive, not at liberty.

He found that he was considered by his friend Harville an engaged man. The Harvilles entertained not a doubt of a mutual attachment between him and Louisa; and though this to a degree was contradicted instantly, it yet made him feel that perhaps by *her* family, by everybody, by *herself* even, the same idea might be held, and that he was not *free* in honour, though if such were to be the conclusion, too free alas! in heart. He had never thought justly on this subject before, and he had not sufficiently considered that his excessive intimacy at Uppercross must have its danger of ill consequence in many ways; and that while trying whether he could attach himself to either of the girls, he might be exciting unpleasant reports if not raising unrequited regard.

He found too late that he had entangled himself, and that precisely as he became thoroughly satisfied of his not *caring* for Louisa at all, he must regard himself as bound to her if her feelings for him were what the Harvilles supposed. It determined him to leave Lyme, and await her perfect recovery elsewhere. He would gladly weaken by any *fair* means whatever sentiment or speculations concerning them might exist; and he went therefore into Shropshire, meaning after a while to return to the Crofts at Kellynch, and act as he found requisite.

He had remained in Shropshire, lamenting the blindness of his own pride and the blunders of his own calculations, till at once released from Louisa by the astonishing felicity of her engagement with Benwick.

Bath—Bath had instantly followed in *thought*, and not long after in *fact*. To Bath—to arrive with hope, to be torn by jealousy at the first sight of Mr. Elliot; to experience all the changes of each at the concert; to be miserable by the morning's circumstantial report, to be now more happy than language could express, or any heart but his own be capable of.

He was very eager and very delightful in the description of what he had felt at the concert; the evening seemed to have been made up of exquisite moments. The moment of her stepping forward in the octagon room to speak to him, the moment of Mr. Elliot's appearing and tearing her away, and one or two subsequent moments, marked by returning hope or increasing despondency, were dwelt on with energy.

'To see you,' cried he, 'in the midst of those who could not be my well-wishers; to see your cousin close by you, conversing and smiling, and feel all the horrible eligibilities and proprieties of the match! To consider it as the certain wish of every being who could hope to influence you! Even if your own feelings were reluctant or indifferent, to consider what powerful support would be his! Was it not enough to make the fool of me which I appeared? How could I look on without agony? Was not the very sight of the friend who sat behind you; was not the recollection of what had been, the knowledge of her influence, the indelible, immovable impression of what persuasion had once done— was it not all against me?'

'You should have distinguished,' replied Anne. 'You should not have suspected me now; the case so different, and my age so different. If I was wrong in yielding to persuasion once, remember it was to persuasion exerted on the side of safety, not of risk. When I yielded, I thought it was to duty; but no duty could be called in aid here. In marrying a man indifferent to me, all risk would have been incurred, and all duty violated.'

'Perhaps I ought to have reasoned thus,' he replied; 'but I could not. I could not derive benefit from the late knowledge I had acquired of your character. I could not bring it into play; it was overwhelmed, buried, lost in those earlier feelings which I had been smarting under year after year. I could think of you only as one who had yielded, who had given me up, who had been influenced by anyone rather than by me. I saw you with the very person who had guided you in that year of misery. I had no reason to believe her of less authority now. The force of habit was to be added.'

'I should have thought,' said Anne, 'that my manner to yourself might have spared you much or all of this.'

'No, no! Your manner might be only the ease which your engagement to another man would give. I left you in this belief; and yet—I was determined to see you again. My spirits rallied with the morning, and I felt that I had still a motive for remaining here. The Admiral's news, indeed, was a revulsion; since that moment I have been divided what to do, and had it been confirmed, this would have been my last day in Bath.'

There was time for all this to pass, with such interruptions only as enhanced the charm of the communication, and Bath could hardly contain any other two beings at once so rationally and so rapturously happy as during that evening occupied the sofa of Mrs. Croft's drawing-room in Gay Street.

Captain Wentworth had taken care to meet the Admiral as he returned into the house, to satisfy him as to Mr. Elliot and Kellynch; and the delicacy of the Admiral's good-nature kept him from saying another word on the subject to Anne. He was quite concerned lest he might have been giving her pain by touching on a tender part—who could say? She might be liking her cousin better than he liked her; and, upon recollection, if they had been to marry at all, why should they have waited so long? When the evening closed, it is probable that the Admiral received some new ideas from his wife, whose particularly friendly manner in parting with her gave Anne the gratifying persuasion of her seeing and approving. It had been such a day to Anne; the hours which had passed since her leaving Camden Place had done so much! She was almost bewildered—almost too happy in looking back. It was necessary to sit up half the night, and lie awake the remainder, to comprehend with composure her present state, and pay for the overplus of bliss by headache and fatigue.

Then follows Chapter XI., *i.e.* XII. in the published book and at the end is written—

Finis, July 18, 1816.

Chapter XIII

The Last Work.

JANE AUSTEN WAS TAKEN from us: how much unexhausted talent perished with her, how largely she might yet have contributed to the entertainment of her readers, if her life had been prolonged, cannot be known; but it is certain that the mine at which she had so long laboured was not worked out, and that she was still diligently employed in collecting fresh materials from it. *Persuasion* had been finished in August 1816; some time was probably given to correcting it for the press; but on the 27th of the following January, according to the date on her own manuscript, she began a new novel, and worked at it up to the 17th of March. The chief part of this manuscript is written in her usual firm and neat hand, but some of the latter pages seem to have been first traced in pencil, probably when she was too weak to sit long at her desk, and written over in ink afterwards. The quantity produced does not indicate any decline of power or industry, for in those seven weeks twelve chapters had been completed. It is more difficult to judge of the quality of a work so little advanced. It had received no name; there was scarcely any indication what the course of the story was to be, nor was any heroine yet perceptible, who, like Fanny Price, or Anne Elliot, might draw round her the sympathies of the reader. Such an unfinished fragment cannot be presented to the public; but I am persuaded that some of Jane Austen's admirers will be glad to learn something about the latest creations which were forming themselves in her mind; and therefore, as some of the principal characters were already sketched in with a vigorous hand, I will try to give an idea of them, illustrated by extracts from the work.

The scene is laid at Sanditon, a village on the Sussex coast, just struggling into notoriety as a bathing-place, under the patronage of the two principal proprietors of the parish, Mr. Parker and Lady Denham.

Mr. Parker was an amiable man, with more enthusiasm than judgment, whose somewhat shallow mind overflowed with the one idea of the prosperity of Sanditon, together with a jealous contempt of the rival village of Brinshore, where a similar attempt was going on. To the regret of his much-enduring wife, he had left his family mansion, with all its ancestral comforts of gardens, shrubberies, and shelter, situated in a valley some miles inland, and had built a new residence—a Trafalgar House—on the bare brow of the hill overlooking Sanditon and the sea, exposed to every wind that blows; but he will confess to no discomforts, nor suffer his family to feel any from the change. The following extract brings him before the reader, mounted on his hobby:—

'He wanted to secure the promise of a visit, and to get as many of the family as his own house would hold to follow him to Sanditon as soon as possible; and, healthy as all the Heywoods undeniably were, he foresaw that every one of them would be benefitted by the sea. He held it indeed as certain that no person, however upheld for the present by fortuitous aids of exercise and spirit in a semblance of health, could be really in a state of secure and permanent health without spending at least six weeks by the sea every year. The sea air and sea-bathing together were nearly infallible; one or other of them being a match for every disorder of the stomach, the lungs, or the blood. They were antispasmodic, anti-pulmonary, anti-bilious, and anti-rheumatic. Nobody could catch cold by the sea; nobody wanted appetite by the sea; nobody wanted spirits; nobody wanted strength. They were healing, softening, relaxing, fortifying, and bracing, seemingly just as was wanted; sometimes one, sometimes the other. If the sea breeze failed, the seabath was the certain corrective; and when bathing disagreed, the sea breeze was evidently designed by nature for the cure. His eloquence, however, could not prevail. Mr. and Mrs. Heywood never left home … The maintenance, education, and fitting out of fourteen children demanded a very quiet, settled, careful course of life; and obliged them to be stationary and healthy at Willingden. What prudence had at first enjoined was now rendered pleasant by habit. They never left home, and they had a gratification in saying so.'

Lady Denham's was a very different character. She was a rich vulgar widow, with a sharp but narrow mind, who cared for the prosperity of Sanditon only so far as it might increase the value of her own property. She is thus described:—

'Lady Denham had been a rich Miss Brereton, born to wealth, but not to education. Her first husband had been a Mr. Hollis, a man of considerable property in the country, of which a large share of the parish of Sanditon, with manor and mansion-house, formed a part. He had been an elderly man when she married him; her own age about thirty.

Her motives for such a match could be little understood at the distance of forty years, but she had so well nursed and pleased Mr. Hollis that at his death he left her everything—all his estates, and all at her disposal. After a widowhood of some years she had been induced to marry again. The late Sir Harry Denham, of Denham Park, in the neighbourhood of Sanditon, succeeded in removing her and her large income to his own domains; but he could not succeed in the views of permanently enriching his family which were attributed to him. She had been too wary to put anything out of her own power, and when, on Sir Harry's death, she returned again to her own house at Sanditon, she was said to have made this boast, "that though she had *got* nothing but her title from the family, yet she had *given* nothing for it." For the title it was to be supposed that she married.

'Lady Denham was indeed a great lady, beyond the common wants of society; for she had many thousands a year to bequeath, and three distinct sets of people to be courted by:—her own relations, who might very reasonably wish for her original thirty thousand pounds among them; the legal heirs of Mr. Hollis, who might hope to be more indebted to *her* sense of justice than he had allowed them to be to *his*; and those members of the Denham family for whom her second husband had hoped to make a good bargain. By all these, or by branches of them, she had, no doubt, been long and still continued to be well attacked; and of these three divisions Mr. Parker did not hesitate to say that Mr. Hollis's kindred were the least in favour, and Sir Harry Denham's the most. The former, he believed, had done themselves irremediable harm by expressions of very unwise resentment at the time of Mr. Hollis's death: the latter, to the advantage of being the remnant of a connection which she certainly valued, joined those of having been known to her from their childhood, and of being always at hand to pursue their interests by seasonable attentions. But another claimant was now to be taken into account: a young female relation whom Lady Denham had been induced to receive into her family. After having always protested against any such addition, and often enjoyed the repeated defeat she had given to every attempt of her own relations to introduce 'this young lady, or that young lady,' as a companion at Sanditon House, she had brought back with her from London last Michaelmas a Miss Clara Brereton, who bid fair to vie in favour with Sir Edward Denham, and to secure for herself and her family that share of the accumulated property which they had certainly the best right to inherit.'

Lady Denham's character comes out in a conversation which takes place at Mr. Parker's tea-table.

'The conversation turned entirely upon Sanditon, its present number of visitants, and the chances of a good season. It was evident that Lady Denham had more anxiety, more fears of loss than her coadjutor. She wanted to have the place fill faster, and seemed to have many harassing apprehensions of the lodgings being in some instances underlet. To a report that a large boarding-school was expected she replies, 'Ah, well, no harm in that. They will stay their six weeks, and out of such a number who knows but some may be consumptive, and want asses' milk; and I have two milch asses at this very time. But perhaps the little Misses may hurt the furniture. I hope they will have a good sharp governess to look after them.' But she wholly disapproved of Mr. Parker's wish to secure the residence of a medical man amongst them. 'Why, what should we do with a doctor here? It would only be encouraging our servants and the poor to fancy themselves ill, if there was a doctor at hand. Oh, pray let us have none of that tribe at Sanditon: we go on very well as we are. There is the sea, and the downs, and my milch asses: and I have told Mrs. Whitby that if anybody enquires for a chamber horse, they may be supplied at a fair rate (poor Mr. Hollis's chamber horse, as good as new); and what can people want more? I have lived seventy good years in the world, and never took physic, except twice: and never saw the face of a doctor in all my life on my own account; and I really believe if my poor dear Sir Harry had never seen one neither, he would have been alive now. Ten fees, one after another, did the men take who sent him out of the world. I beseech you, Mr. Parker, no doctors here.'

This lady's character comes out more strongly in a conversation with Mr. Parker's guest, Miss Charlotte Heywood. Sir Edward Denham with his sister Esther and Clara Brereton have just left them.

'Charlotte accepted an invitation from Lady Denham to remain with her on the terrace, when the others adjourned to the library. Lady Denham, like a true great lady, talked, and talked only of her own concerns, and Charlotte listened. Taking hold of Charlotte's arm with the ease of one who felt that any notice from her was a favour, and communicative from the same sense of importance, or from a natural love of talking, she immediately said in a tone of great satisfaction, and with a look of arch sagacity:—

'Miss Esther wants me to invite her and her brother to spend a week with me at Sanditon House, as I did last summer, but I shan't. She has been trying to get round me every way with her praise of this and her praise of that; but I saw what she was about. I saw through it all. I am not very easily taken in, my dear.'

Charlotte could think of nothing more harmless to be said than the simple enquiry of, 'Sir Edward and Miss Denham?'

'Yes, my dear; *my young folks*, as I call them, sometimes: for I take them very much by the hand, and had them with me last summer, about this time, for a week—from Monday to Monday—and very delighted and thankful they were. For they are very good young people, my dear. I would not have you think that I only notice them for poor dear Sir Harry's sake. No, no; they are very deserving themselves, or, trust me, they would not be so much in my company. I am not the woman to help anybody blindfold. I always take care to know what I am about, and who I have to deal with before I stir a finger. I do not think I was ever overreached in my life; and that is a good deal for a woman to say that has been twice married. Poor dear Sir Harry (between ourselves) thought at first to have got more, but (with a bit of a sigh) he is gone, and we must not find fault with the dead. Nobody could live happier together than us: and he was a very honourable man, quite the gentleman, of ancient family; and when he died I gave Sir Edward his gold watch.'

This was said with a look at her companion which implied its right to produce a great impression; and seeing no rapturous astonishment in Charlotte's countenance, she added quickly,

'He did not bequeath it to his nephew, my dear; it was no bequest; it was not in the will. He only told me, and *that* but *once*, that he should wish his nephew to have his watch; but it need not have been binding, if I had not chose it.'

'Very kind indeed, very handsome!' said Charlotte, absolutely forced to affect admiration.

'Yes, my dear; and it is not the only kind thing I have done by him. I have been a very liberal friend to Sir Edward; and, poor young man, he needs it bad enough. For, though I am only the dowager, my dear, and he is the heir, things do not stand between us in the way they usually do between those two parties. Not a shilling do I receive from the Denham estate. Sir Edward has no payments to make *me*. *He* don't stand uppermost, believe me; it is *I* that help *him*.'

'Indeed! he is a very fine young man, and particularly elegant in his address.'

This was said chiefly for the sake of saying something; but Charlotte directly saw that it was laying her open to suspicion, by Lady Denham's giving a shrewd glance at her, and replying,

'Yes, yes; he's very well to look at; and it is to be hoped that somebody of large fortune will think so; for Sir Edward *must* marry for money. He and I often talk that matter over. A handsome young man like him will go smirking and smiling about, and paying girls compliments, but he knows he *must* marry for money. And Sir Edward is a very steady young man, in the main, and has got very good notions.'

'Sir Edward Denham,' said Charlotte, 'with such personal advantages, may be almost sure of getting a woman of fortune, if he chooses it.'

This glorious sentiment seemed quite to remove suspicion.

'Aye, my dear, that is very sensibly said; and if we could but get a young heiress to Sanditon! But heiresses are monstrous scarce! I do not think we have had an heiress here, nor even a *Co.*, since Sanditon has been a public place. Families come after families, but, as far as I can learn, it is not one in a hundred of them that have any real property, landed or funded. An income, perhaps, but no property. Clergymen, may be, or lawyers from town, or half-pay officers, or widows with only a jointure; and what good can such people do to anybody? Except just as they take our empty houses, and (between ourselves) I think they are great fools for not staying at home. Now, if we could get a young heiress to be sent here for her health, and, as soon as she got well, have her fall in love with Sir Edward! And Miss Esther must marry somebody of fortune, too. She must get a rich husband. Ah! young ladies that have no money are very much to be pitied.' After a short pause: 'If Miss Esther thinks to talk me into inviting them to come and stay at Sanditon House, she will find herself mistaken. Matters are altered with me since last summer, you know: I have Miss Clara with me now, which makes a great difference. I should not choose to have my two housemaid's time taken up all the morning in dusting out bedrooms. They have Miss Clara's room to put to rights, as well as mine, every day. If they had hard work, they would want higher wages.'

Charlotte's feelings were divided between amusement and indignation. She kept her countenance, and kept a civil silence; but without attempting to listen any longer, and only conscious that Lady Denham was still talking in the same way, allowed her own thoughts to form themselves into such meditation as this:—'She is thoroughly mean; I had no expectation of anything so bad. Mr. Parker spoke too mildly of her. He is too kind-hearted to see clearly, and their very connection misleads him. He has persuaded her to engage in the same speculation, and because they have so far the same object in view, he fancies that she feels like him in other things; but she is very, very mean. I can see no good in her. Poor Miss Brereton! And it makes everybody mean about her. This poor Sir Edward and his sister! how far nature meant them to be respectable I cannot tell; but they are obliged to be mean in their servility to her; and I am mean, too, in giving her my attention with the appearance of coinciding with her. Thus it is when rich people are sordid.'

Mr. Parker has two unmarried sisters of singular character. They live together; Diana, the younger, always takes the lead, and the elder follows in the same track. It is their pleasure to fancy themselves invalids to a degree and in a manner never experienced by others; but, from a state of exquisite pain and utter prostration, Diana Parker can always rise to be officious in the concerns of all her acquaintance, and to make incredible exertions where they are not wanted.

It would seem that they must be always either very busy for the good of others, or else extremely ill themselves. Some natural delicacy of constitution, in fact, with an unfortunate turn for medicine, especially quack medicine, had given them an early tendency at various times to various disorders. The rest of their suffering was from their own fancy, the love of distinction, and the love of the wonderful. They had charitable hearts and many amiable feelings; but a spirit of restless activity, and the glory of doing more than anybody else, had a share in every exertion of benevolence, and there was vanity in all they did, as well as in all they endured.

These peculiarities come out in the following letter of Diana Parker to her brother:—

'My Dear Tom,—We were much grieved at your accident, and if you had not described yourself as having fallen into such very good hands, I should have been with you at all hazards the day after receipt of your letter, though it found me suffering under a more severe attack than usual of my old grievance, spasmodic bile, and hardly able to crawl from my bed to the sofa. But how were you treated? Send me more particulars in your next. If indeed a simple sprain, as you denominate it, nothing would have been so judicious as friction—friction by the hand alone, supposing it could be applied *immediately*. Two years ago I happened to be calling on Mrs. Sheldon, when her coachman sprained his foot, as he was cleaning the carriage, and could hardly limp into the house; but by the immediate use of friction alone, steadily persevered in (I rubbed his ancle with my own hands for four hours without inter-mission), he was well in three days ... Pray never run into peril again in looking for an apothecary on our account; for had you the most experi-enced man in his line settled at Sanditon, it would be no recommenda-tion to us. We have entirely done with the whole medical tribe. We have consulted physician after physician in vain, till we are quite convinced that they can do nothing for us, and that we must trust to our knowl-edge of our own wretched constitutions for any relief; but if you think it advisable for the interests of the *place* to get a medical man there, I will undertake the commission with pleasure, and have no doubt of suc-ceeding. I could soon put the necessary irons in the fire. As for getting to Sanditon myself, it is an impossibility. I grieve to say that I cannot attempt it, but my feelings tell me too plainly that in my present state the sea-air would probably be the death of me; and in truth I doubt whether Susan's nerves would be equal to the effort. She has been suf-fering much from headache, and six leeches a day, for ten days together, relieved her so little that we thought it right to change our measures; and being convinced on examination that much of the evil lay in her gums, I persuaded her to attack the disorder there. She has accordingly had three teeth drawn, and is decidedly better; but her nerves are a good deal deranged, she can only speak in a whisper, and fainted away this morning on poor Arthur's trying to suppress a cough.'

Within a week of the date of this letter, in spite of the impossibility of moving, and of the fatal effects to be apprehended from the sea-air, Diana Parker was at Sanditon with her sister. She had flattered her-self that by her own indefatigable exertions, and by setting at work the agency of many friends, she had induced two large families to take houses at Sanditon. It was to expedite these politic views that she came;

and though she met with some disappointment of her expectation, yet she did not suffer in health.

Such were some of the *dramatis personæ*, ready dressed and prepared for their parts. They are at least original and unlike any that the author had produced before. The success of the piece must have depended on the skill with which these parts might be played; but few will be inclined to distrust the skill of one who had so often succeeded. If the author had lived to complete her work, it is probable that these personages might have grown into as mature an individuality of character, and have taken as permanent a place amongst our familiar acquaintance, as Mr. Bennet, or John Thorp, Mary Musgrove, or Aunt Norris herself.

Chapter XIV

Postscript.

WHEN FIRST I WAS asked to put together a memoir of my aunt, I saw reasons for declining the attempt. It was not only that, having passed the three score years and ten usually allotted to man's strength, and being unaccustomed to write for publication, I might well distrust my ability to complete the work, but that I also knew the extreme scantiness of the materials out of which it must be constructed. The grave closed over my aunt fifty-two years ago; and during that long period no idea of writing her life had been entertained by any of her family. Her nearest relatives, far from making provision for such a purpose, had actually destroyed many of the letters and papers by which it might have been facilitated. They were influenced, I believe, partly by an extreme dislike to publishing private details, and partly by never having assumed that the world would take so strong and abiding an interest in her works as to claim her name as public property. It was therefore necessary for me to draw upon recollections rather than on written documents for my materials; while the subject itself supplied me with nothing striking or prominent with which to arrest the attention of the reader. It has been said that the happiest individuals, like nations during their happiest periods, have no history. In the case of my aunt, it was not only that her course of life was unvaried, but that her own disposition was remarkably calm and even. There was in her nothing eccentric or angular; no ruggedness of temper; no singularity of manner; none of the morbid sensibility or exaggeration of feeling, which not unfrequently accompanies great talents, to be worked up into a picture. Hers was a mind well balanced on a basis of good sense, sweetened by an affectionate heart, and regulated by fixed principles; so that she was to be distinguished from many other amiable and sensible women only by that peculiar genius which shines out clearly enough in her works, but of which a biographer can make little use. The motive which at last induced me to make the attempt is exactly expressed in the passage prefixed to these pages. I thought that I saw something to be done: knew of no one who could do it but myself, and so was driven to the enterprise. I am glad that I have been able to finish my work. As a family record it can scarcely fail to be interesting to those relatives who must ever set a high value on their connection with Jane Austen, and to them I especially dedicate it; but as I have been asked to do so, I also submit it to the censure of the public, with all its faults both of deficiency and redundancy. I know that its value in their eyes must depend, not on any merits of its own, but on the degree of estimation in which my aunt's works may still be held; and indeed I shall esteem it one of the strongest testimonies ever borne to her talents, if for her sake an interest can be taken in so poor a sketch as I have been able to draw.

Bray Vicarage:

Sept. 7, 1869.

Postscript printed at the end of the first edition; omitted from the second.

Since these pages were in type, I have read with astonishment the strange misrepresentation of my aunt's manners given by Miss Mitford in a letter which appears in her lately-published *Life*, vol. i. p. 305. Miss Mitford does not profess to have known Jane Austen herself, but to report what had been told her by her mother. Having stated that her mother '*before her marriage*' was well acquainted with Jane Austen and her family, she writes thus:—'Mamma says that she was *then* the prettiest, silliest, most affected, husband-hunting butterfly she ever remembers.' The editor of Miss Mitford's Life very properly observes in a note how different this description is from 'every other account of Jane Austen from whatever quarter.' Certainly it is so totally at variance with the modest simplicity of character which I have attributed to my aunt, that if it could be supposed to have a semblance of truth, it must be equally injurious to her memory and to my trustworthiness as her biographer. Fortunately I am not driven to put my authority in competition with that of Miss Mitford, nor to ask which ought to be considered the better witness in this case; because I am able to prove by a reference to dates that Miss Mitford must have been under a mistake, and that her mother could not possibly have known what she was supposed to have reported; inasmuch as Jane Austen, at the time referred to, was a little girl.

Mrs. Mitford was the daughter of Dr. Russell, Rector of Ashe, a parish adjoining Steventon, so that the families of Austen and Russell must at that time have been known to each other. But the date assigned by

Miss Mitford for the termination of the acquaintance is the time of her mother's marriage. This took place in October 1785, when Jane, who had been born in December 1775, was not quite ten years old. In point of fact, however, Miss Russell's opportunities of observing Jane Austen must have come to an end still earlier: for upon Dr. Russell's death, in January 1783, his widow and daughter removed from the neighbour-hood, so that all intercourse between the families ceased when Jane was little more than seven years old.

All persons who undertake to narrate from hearsay things which are supposed to have taken place before they were born are liable to error, and are apt to call in imagination to the aid of memory: and hence it arises that many a fancy piece has been substituted for genuine history.

I do not care to correct the inaccurate account of Jane Austen's manners in after life: because Miss Mitford candidly expresses a doubt whether she had not been misinformed on that point.

Nov. 17, 1869.

A 2005 PHOTOGRAPH OF JANE AUSTEN'S HOUSE IN CHAWTON

William Austen — Rebecca Walter
(1701–1737)   (née Hampson)

Tysoe Saul Hancock — Philadelphia
(d. 1775)   (1730–1792)

Jean Capot de Feuillide — Eliza   Henry
(guillotined 1794)   (Elizabeth)   Austen
                      (1761–1813)

Rev. George — Cassandra Leigh
(1731–1805)   (1739–1827)

Leonora
(1732–1783)

Rev. James   George   Edward   Henry
(1765–1819)   (1766–1838)   (1767–1852)   (1771–1850)

Cassandra   Francis   Jane   Charles
(1773–1845)   (1774–1865)   (1775–1817)   (1779–1852)

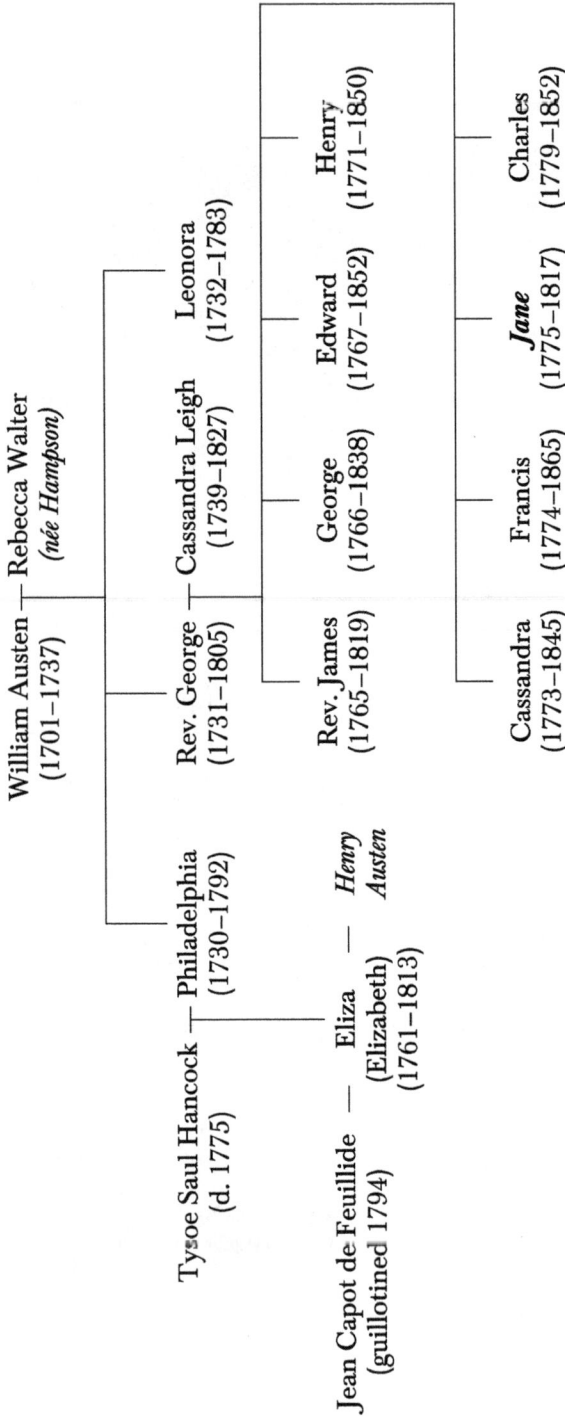

WILLIAM AUSTEN'S FAMILY TREE:
TWO GENERATIONS

Rev. George — Cassandra Leigh
(1731–1805)   (1739–1827)

(1) Rev. James (1765–1819)

Anne Matthew (d. 1795)

Anna (1793–1872)

(2) Mary Lloyd (1771–1843)

Rev. James Edward Austen-*Leigh* (1798–1874)

Caroline Mary *Craven* (1805–1880)

Edward *Knight* (1767–1852) — Elizabeth *Bridges*

Fanny (1793–1882)
Edward (1794–1879)
George (1795–1867)
Henry (1797–1843)
William (1798–1873)
Elizabeth (1800–1884)
Marianne (1801–1896)
Charles (1803–1867)
Louisa (1804–1889)
Cassandra Jane (1806–1842)
Brook John (1808–1878)

(Sir) Francis (1774–1865) — Mary Gibson

Mary Jane (1807–1836)
Francis William (1809–1858)
Henry Edgar (1811–1854)
George (1812–1903)
Cassandra Eliza (1814–1849)
Herbert Grey (1815–1888)
Elizabeth (1817–1830)
Catherine Anne (1818–1877)
Edward Thomas (1820–1908)
Frances Sophia (1821–1904)
Cholmely (1823–1824)

Frances Palmer (1) — Charles (1779–1852) (2)

Cassandra Esten (1808–1897)
Harriet Jane (1810–1865)
Frances Palmer (1812–1882)
Elizabeth (b. & d. 1814)

Harriet Palmer

Charles John (1821–1867)
George (1822–1824)
Jane (1824–1825)
Henry (1826–1851)

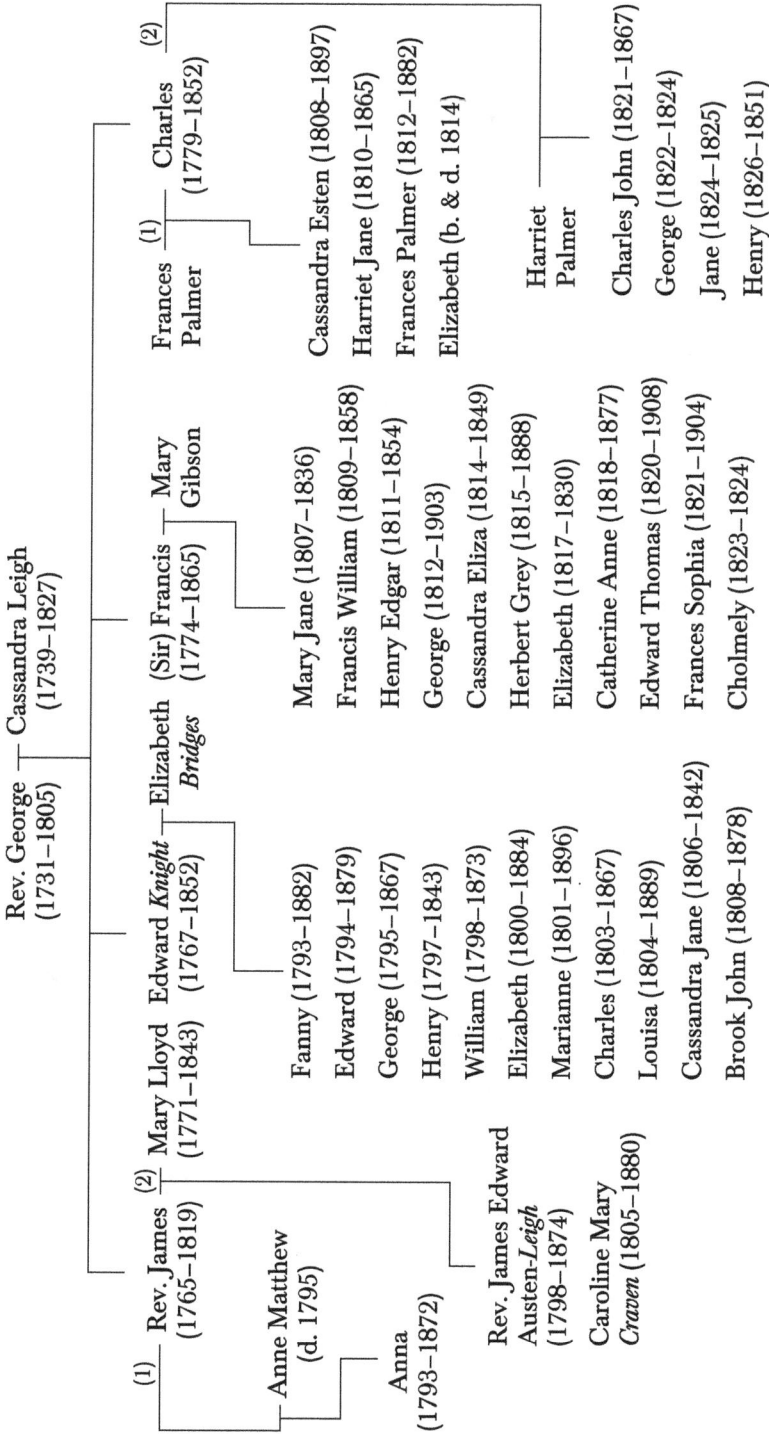

JANE AUSTEN'S NEPHEWS AND NIECES

143

SELECTED WORKS OF JANE AUSTEN

NOVELS

Sense and Sensibility (1811)

Pride and Prejudice (1813)

Mansfield Park (1814)

Emma (1815)

Northanger Abbey (1818, posthumous)

Persuasion (1818, posthumous)

SHORT FICTION

Lady Susan (1794, 1805)

UNFINISHED FICTION

The Watsons (1804)

Sanditon (1817)

OTHER WORKS

Sir Charles Grandison (adapted play) (1793, 1800)

Plan of a Novel (1815)

Poems (1796–1817)

Prayers (1796–1817)

Letters (1796–1817)

www.ingramcontent.com/pod-product-compliance
Lightning Source LLC
Chambersburg PA
CBHW060816100426
42813CB00004B/1098